FOREWORD

The region comprising the Mexican states of Campeche, Chiapas, Quintana Roo, Tabasco and Yucatán, and the Central American countries of Belize, El Salvador, Guatemala and Honduras, was home to one of the most important cultures in the ancient world - the Maya.

The Maya civilization defies analysis: for every doubt resolved, new questions arise. As time goes on and specialists delve into its mysteries, new findings emerge that renew their enthusiasm for this endlessly fascinating people.

This book provides a general overview of the area known as the Maya World from its cultural background and origins to its decline. The author offers a summary of its principal scientific, astronomical, architectural and artistic achievements. He describes the major cities, and mentions their most important temples, palaces and pyramids. To facilitate the journey through the Maya World, explanations are given on a state-by-state, country-by-country basis.

Reference is made to the first explorers who not only paved the way for new generations of scholars but also for ordinary visitors since, thanks to them, we can appreciate the marvels of this culture as we walk the paths that the builders of these monumental cities trod thousands of years ago.

We hope that this book will encourage those who have already had the opportunity of visiting these cities to find out more about this marvelous people and inspire those who have not already done so to discover it for themselves. Fortunately, the Maya World is now accessible to all.

Víctor Vera Castillo

Tikal, Guatemala

Palenque, Chiapas, Mexico

Tulum, Quintana Roo, Mexico

DIRECTORY

EDITORIAL DANTE

Calle 17 No. 138-B, por Prolongación Paseo de Montejo, Colonia Itzimná
Email: sacdante@sureste.com
Mérida, Yucatán 97100, México.
(99) 44-9994

ISBN 970-605-124-4

VICTOR VERA THANKS:

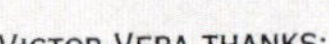

Editorial: Joanna Green, Ester Bejar, Susanna Trejo. Design: Tania Vera, Mario Sánchez, Hugo Rojas. Photography: Ignacio Guevara, Adalberto Ríos S., David Baeza, Gonzalo I. Arcila, Fulvio Eccardi, Editorial Raíces, Gonzalo Infante, José Antonio Granados, Ricardo Mata, Michel Zabé, Secretaría de Turismo de Tabasco, Secretaría de Turismo de Chiapas, Vicente Murphy, Tony Rath

Editorial Verás. Calle Liebre No. 16, SM 20, Cancún, Quintana Roo, México, C.P. 77500; Tel.: (9) 884-1106, Fax: (9) 884-4728. email: everas@cancun.com.mx
website: ektourscoleccionveras.com

CONTENTS

MAPS

TABASCO 46

CHIAPAS 50

CAMPECHE 60

YUCATÁN 68

QUINTANA ROO 86

BELIZE 100

GUATEMALA 108

EL SALVADOR 118

HONDURAS 120

GETTING AROUND 126

Previous photo: Equinox in Dzibilchaltún, Yucatán

SETTLEMENT

During the Ice Age, Asian man migrated towards the American continent through the Bering Straits, pursuing the large animals (mammoth and bison) that formed the basis of his diet; the greatest human influx occurred during the Wisconsin (70,000-25,000 B.C.). He continued his descent towards the southwest of the United States through an ice-free corridor that formed in the Rockies.

Nomadic hunters from North America entered Mexico approximately 20,000 years ago (the Tepexpan man, in the state of Mexico; Santa Isabel Ixtapan; Tehuacan, Puebla). They survived by hunting large animals (mastodons, etc.) and gathering plants, nuts, seeds, tubers and fruit from the wild. In approximately 7000 B´.C., the climatic changes that affected the land led to the extinction of the megafauna and encouraged agriculture, thereby establishing the bases for subsequent development.

MAN ENTERS THE MAYA WORLD

In the Maya region, evidence of the earliest occupation has been found in Chiapas, Guatemala, the coastal area of Belize and the Loltún Caves, in Yucatán (8000 B.C.). With a basic hunting-and-gathering economy, these micro-groups sought areas that would supply the raw materials for their flint tools. This has been corroborated in Santa Marta and Teopisca, Chiapas, Los Tapiales in Guatemala and the coastal area of Belize.

Between 3000 and 1000 B.C., migrant groups reached the Gulf Coast. These semi-sedentary macro-groups introduced the earliest forms of agriculture and established the first villages and pottery complexes of Chiapas and Guatemala (Barra y Ocós) and Cuello, creating the basis for their subsequent development in Belize.

Blom Plate, Altun-Há, Belize

THE MAYA BOOK OF CREATION

According to the Popol Vuh, the sacred book of creation of the Quiché Maya, the gods shaped the first man out of clay, "but he was soft, and lacked movement." The next man was carved out of wood, "he spoke, but had no soul, he did not remember his Creator,"; his punishment was to be destroyed by a flood. Later, the gods agreed that man would be made from maize. This man acknowledged his creators and thanked them for giving him life.

The Popol Vuh was discovered by Father Francisco Jiménez in Chichicastenango, Guatemala, in the 18th century. It is believed to have been written after the Conquest, yet drawn from ancient sources. Even today, maize is the sacred food of the Maya.

PERIODS OF MAYA CIVILIZATION

PRECLASSIC (1800 B.C.- A.D. 250)
This was the time of Olmec influence, the first villages, agriculture and the construction of ceremonial centers. The nobility were buried in chambers inside mounds, and were surrounded by rich offerings. This period saw an intensification of the trade in both luxury and utility goods.

CLASSIC (A.D. 250-900)
During the Classic period Mayan culture reached its peak. There was greater economic development, an increase in the construction of ceremonial centers and art in all its manifestations: sculpture, stucco and painting all flourished. Social division was accentuated. The power of the ruling social class was exercised in the economy and politics through religion. Science made great advances. At the end of the period, cities in the lowland areas of Chiapas and Guatemala were abandoned for reasons as yet unknown.

POST-CLASSIC (A.D. 900-1524)
The conquest of Chichén Itzá, Mayapan and Uxmal (Yucatán) by "Mexicanized" Maya possibly hailing from the Gulf Coast marked a great cultural change. The predominance of militarism led to the emergence of new gods and forms of worship, and artistic styles emerged combining Maya and Toltec features. Following various struggles for power, around A.D. 1200, a weakened Chichén Itzá was conquered by Mayapán, a city which subsequently controlled the Yucatán until its own downfall in 1441. The Peninsula split into city states and war broke out.

In the highlands of Chiapas and Guatemala, the Maya were vassals of the Aztecs of Central Mexico.

Mesoamerican cultures

Mesoamerica comprises the territory between the Lerma & Pánuco rivers (Mexico), and the Ulúa River Valley (Honduras)

MESOAMERICA

The Mesoamerican cultural area is defined by the analysis and comparison of historical and cultural elements. It includes the territory between the Lerma and Pánuco rivers (Mexico) to the north and the valley of the Ulúa river (Honduras) to the south. The cultures that developed in the region shared the use of the huipil and loincloth, the planting stick for sowing seeds and the cultivation of beans, squash, chili and corn. Other common features include the pyramidal bases crowned with temples and the ballgame. They were governed by a solar calendar of 365 days plus five fateful days and a 260-day ritual calendar.

OLMEC

Olmec culture ("in the place of rubber") developed from 1700 B.C. to 200 B.C. Its influence was felt throughout Mesoamerica. The nucleus of this culture was the border between the states of Veracruz and Tabasco. Their sculptures reveal their veneration of the jaguar and the serpent. They initiated the architectural tradition of building pyramidal bases around open plazas built on a north-south axis.

TULA

Tula ("the place of marsh sedge"), the city that inherited aspects of the Teotihuacán culture and developed between A.D. 700 and 1250, worshipped the god Quetzalcóatl through the morning star (Venus), Xólotl (the god of the underworld) and Ehécatl (the god of the wind). Its architectural contributions include serpentine columns, Atlanteans, processions of priests, halls supported by columns, tzompantli (buildings crowned by skull racks) and coatepantli (walls of serpents).

Olmec figurine

Temple of Quetzalcóatl, Teotihuacán, Mexico

TEOTIHUACÁN

Magnificent city (20 sq. km) located north of Mexico City, dated between 400 B.C. and A.D. 700. Teotihuacán ("place of gods") contained ceremonial centers, housing districts for craftsmen and schools. Their principal gods were Tláloc (the god of water), Quetzalcóatl (plumed serpent), Mictlantecuhtli (lord of the Underworld) and Xiuhtecuhtli (god of fire). Teotihuacan was defeated by Cholula.

ZAPOTEC & MIXTEC

The foundation of Monte Albán marked the start of Zapotec hegemony for over a thousand years (A.D. 500-1521) in the Valley of Oaxaca. It was characterized by its fine manufacture of codices, elaborate pottery and construction of monumental buildings. On their tombs, the Zapotecs recorded the images of their rulers in murals, sculptures and carved stones. The Mixtec culture is renowned for its gold artifacts, particularly jewelery.

TOTONAC

This culture developed between A.D. 900 and 1200. Its most important city was El Tajín, which contains the Pyramid of the Niches, decorated with frets and niches complementing the chiaroscuro. It is famous for its monumental pottery sculptures, elegantly dressed figurines, smiling faces, yokes, votive axes and palmas. Examples of its unusual pictorial art can be seen at Las Higueras.

MEXICA OR AZTEC

The city of Tenochtitlán (A.D. 1111-1521) was founded by Chichimeca tribes who migrated to the Valley of Mexico under Huitzilipochtli. The Triple Alliance formed by the chiefdoms of Tenochtitlán, Texcoco and Tacuba consolidated a militaristic empire, which was defeated by the Spaniards during the Conquest. The principal pyramid, the Templo Mayor has a double inscription dedicated to Tláloc and Huitzilopochtli (the lord of war). Mexica art is characterized by its stone and pottery sculptures and alabaster figures.

Atlanteans , Tula, Hidalgo

CRONOLOGY

WORLD

ANCIENT PERIOD

3500-3000 B.C.
Sumarian civilization. Cuneiform writing.
3000-2500
The Sphinx Cheops Pyramid, Egypt.

2772
365-day calendar, Egypt.
753
Rome founded.
700-600
Acropolis, Athens.
335-323
Alexander the Great.

250-215
Wall of China.
168
Beginning of Roman Empire.

50
Emperor Julius Caesar in Rome.
46
Julian Calendar.
0
Dawn of Christian era.

DARK & MIDDLE AGES

476 A.D.
Fall of Roman Empire. Beginning of Dark Ages.
711
Moors invade Spain.

800
Coronation of Charlemagne. Apogee de Machu Picchu in Perú.
1096-1099
First Crusade.

MESOAMERICA

ANCIENT PERIOD

7500 B.C.
Dawn of agriculture.
1300-900 B.C.
Development of Olmec culture.

500
Zapotec civilization Foundation of Monte Albán

(Oaxaca). Evolution of writing in Mesoamerica. Apogee of Cuicuilco.
100
Pyramid of Sun in Teotihuacán.

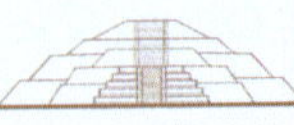

DARK & MIDDLE AGES

700
El Tajín, Xochicalco & Cacaxtla emerge.

500
Rise of Tula.
8th Century
Foundation & expansion of Tenochtitlán.
1325
Aztec Empire flourished.

16-18th CENTURIES

1521
Conquest of Tenochtitlán.
1810
Mexico, Independence struggle begins.

MAYA WORLD

ARCHAIC

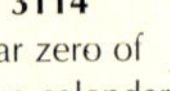

8000-3000 B.C.
First nomadic groups. First settlements: Loltún Caves & Kabah, Yucatán; Santa Marta & Teopisca, Chiapas.

PRE-CLASSIC

3114
Year zero of Mayan calendar.

3000-1000
Migrations from the Gulf of Mexico & the highlands to the Yucatán Peninsula.

Pottery: Barra, Chiapas; Ocós, Guatemala, & Swazey, Belize.
1000-300
Xe pottery. First evidence of the

Mayan culture in Yucatán, Chiapas & Campeche.

300-50
First chiefdoms in Yucatán; Komchén the most important. Kaminaljuyú, the most powerful center in the Southern Highlands. El Mirador & Nakbé dominate the Petén.

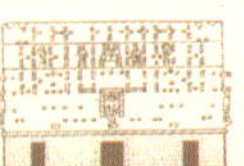

CLASSIC

50 B.C.-250 A.D.
Rise of Tikal & Uaxactún in the Petén. Fortifications in Becán.

250-600 A.D.
In 292 the use of hieroglyphic writing & mathematics began.

Collapse of the Mayan culture in the highlands. Tikal dominates area until 562.
600-900
Great advances in science and art. Rise of Palenque, Yaxchilán & Bonampak in Chiapas; Calakmul &

other centers in the Río Bec area, Campeche;

Uxmal & Kabah

in Yucatán; Caracol in Belize & Copán in Honduras. Tikal dominates the lesser cities of the Petén until the 9th century.

987

16, 17 & 18th CENTURIES

1492 Columbus discovers America.
1513 Vasco Núñez de Balboa spots the

Pacific.
1519 Voyages of Magellan.
1532 Francisco Pizarro begins his campaign to conquer Peru.

1547-1616 Era of Cervantes & Shakespeare.
1770 Industrial Revolution in England.

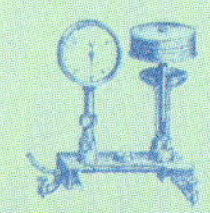

1776 American Independence.
1789 French Revolution.

19th-20th CENTURIES

1821 Independence of Mexico & Central America.
1821-1822 Independence of almost all Latin America.
1858 Benito Juárez President of Mexico.

1910 Start of the Mexican Revolution.
1917 Political Constitution of the United States of Mexico.

1938 Oil industry expropriated.
1968 Student protest movement.

POST-CLASSIC

Foundation of Mayapán.
1007-1200 Chichén Itzá, a powerful Mayan center.
1185-1204

Mayapán replaces Chichén Itzá as capital of the Yucatán Ppeninsula.
1441

16, 17, 18 & 19th CENTURIES

Fall of Mayapán. Tulum & Ichpaatún flourish, in Quintana Roo.
1500

Díaz de Solís & Yáñez Pinzón spot the Yucatecan coast.
1511 Shipwreck of Gonzalo Guerrero, "father of the *mestizaje*" (mixed race).
1517

Expedition of Francisco Hernández de Córdoba.
1518 Expedition of Juan de Grijalva.
1519 Arrival of Hernán Cortés.
1527-1547 Conquest of the Yucatán Peninsula.
1691-1697 Itzae maya defeated at Tayasal, Petén.
1838-1841

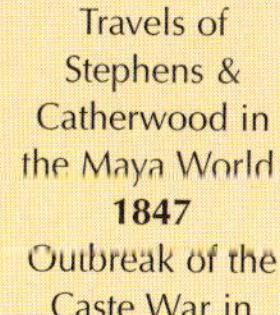

Travels of Stephens & Catherwood in the Maya World.
1847 Outbreak of the Caste War in Yucatán.
1884

Travels of Teobert Maler & Alfred Maudslay.

MAYA WORLD EXPLORERS

The pioneers of Mayan archaeology were a band of 18th and 19th-century explorers who traveled through southeast Mexico and Central America in search of adventure and found the crumbling cities of a long-lost civilization instead. The accounts and drawings they published intrigued the world.

The earliest travelers such as Antonio de Solis (Palenque, 1746), Antonio del Río and Jean Frederic de Waldeck tried to link the cities they visited with the Classical civilizations of the Old World.

Views began to change in the 1840s with the publication of two books written by John L. Stephens who traveled through Central America, Chiapas and the Yucatán in 1841-2. Stephens described his journeys and the 44 ancient sites he explored on the way while his companion Frederick Catherwood produced detailed drawings of the buildings (see later chapters of this book for examples).

Stephens believed that the cities were the legacy of a native civilization and later 19th-century researchers concluded that they were built by the ancient Maya. Armed with cameras, Desiré Charnay, Alfred Maudslay and Teobert Maler visited sites such as Chichén Itzá, Palenque, Tikal and Copán, photographing, mapping and describing them in detail. Their studies were the groundwork for modern Mayan archaeology.

Terns, Quintana Roo

NATURE

Dzitnup Cenote, Yucatán

The Maya World is a land of extraordinary natural diversity. It can be divided into three geographical zones with a variety of ecosystems all incredibly rich in flora and fauna.

The central areas of the Maya World, called the Lowlands corresponds to the Petén region in Guatemala and the basins of the Usumacinta, Grijalva and Motagua rivers. It is a region of abundant rivers, lakes and swamps, its hot humid climate encouraging exuberant forest vegetation.

The northern area includes the Yucatán Peninsula, a plain with no streams or rivers where the climate is extremely hot and, owing to the porosity of the calcareous soil, the water filters down to the sub-soil. In the south there is dense tropical forest, and in the far north, where there is less precipitation, the vegetation is lower and sparser.

The Highlands of Chiapas and Guatemala are dominated by an extensive high plateau with wooded mountain ranges of volcanic origin and valleys. The cold, dry winter climate contrasts with the rainy summers.

Lake Atitlán, Guatemala

ECOSYSTEMS

The Maya World boasts a great diversity of ecosystems, including jungle, cloud forest, temperate forest, mangroves and swamps, savanna, coastal dunes and reefs. The vegetation and wildlife that characterized them are determined by their height above sea level, the climate and the type of soil. During the pre-Hispanic era, the physiognomy of the landscape must have been different, the population was larger and vast areas of forest were cleared for housing and agriculture.

Temperate forest, Chiapas

RIVERS

The majority of the rivers are in the central area and the highlands. The Usumacinta, Grijalva, La Pasión, Candelaria, Nuevo, Hondo, Belize and Motagua rivers were used as transport routes and sources of food, their banks and flood plains were also intensively farmed.

Cloud forest, Guatemala

MOUNTAINS

The Yucatán Peninsula has few hills, except for those in the Puuc region. The mountains in the south of the Lowland region supplied various raw materials. The Highlands comprise a region of enormous mountains (up to 4000 m high), including several active volcanoes. These characteristics facilitated the formation of mineral sources.

OCEANS

The Maya World is flanked by the Pacific Ocean, the Gulf of Mexico, the Caribbean and the Gulf of Honduras. In addition to saltworks, the coast provided access to marine resources. The rivers that flowed into the sea facilitated trade between the Maya coastal and inland cities.

CENOTES

The calcareous soil of the Yucatán Peninsula filters the rainwater that accumulates in underground caverns. As the soil layer retreats and the rock is eroded, underlying water deposits are revealed.

CAVES

Perforations in the ground caused by erosion over thousands of years. Caves and natural wells were regarded as the entrance to the underworld; some were highly venerated.

Ecosystems
1. Jungle
2. Savanna
3. Mangroves
4. Coast
5. Reefs

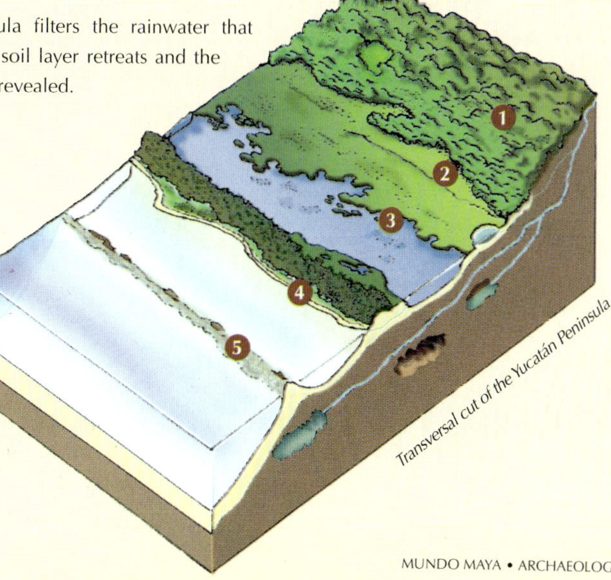

Transversal cut of the Yucatán Peninsula

Copán, Honduras

VEGETATION

Different areas of the Maya World are covered with highland forests, high, medium and low growth jungle, cloud forest, scrub, palm groves, coastal dune vegetation, flood plains, mangrove swamps and marshes. This broad range of vegetation yielded edible fruits and hardwoods used in construction. Herbs were also used for medicinal purposes. In this world of lush vegetation, the Maya coexisted with a variety of animal species, whose flesh provided food and whose skins were used to make clothes. They were familiar with the colors produced by certain plants, clays, insects and sea shells, used to dye textiles and knew how to exploit the the environment to their benefit.

TREES

Some of the most common forest species in the area include the chicozapote tree, which produces the resin used to make balls for the ball game and chewing gum; the breadnut tree, the fruit of which provided food in times of scarcity; the copal tree, used for incense; cacao, whose seeds were used as currency, and which was made into a beverage drunk exclusively by the nobility, and the ceiba, a sacred tree symbolizing Maya cosmogony.

MARSH & FLOODPLAIN VEGETATION

The Maya World has large expanses of permanently flooded land. The most important example in this respect is Tabasco, although marshes are common along the coast of the Yucatán Peninsula and in Belize. The principal vegetation in such areas are logwood stands (palo de tinte), savannas, reedbeds and mangrove swamps.

WILDLIFE BIRDS

The brilliant plumage of parrots, macaws, toucans, herons and hummingbirds was used by the Maya in their clothing and ornamentation. The feathers of the quetzal, a bird native to the cloud forests of the highlands of Guatemala, Chiapas and Honduras, were highly prized. Other species included partridges, quail, doves, great curassows and the famous ocellated turkey, as well as vultures, hawks and eagles.

Left. Representation of a jaguar, Chichén Itzá;
Right. Jaguar from the area

OTHER ANIMALS

The unusual animal life in the forests includes a wide range of species such as agoutis, monkeys, coatimundis, raccoons, skunks, armadillos, kinkajous, peccaries, hare, deer, tapirs, and howler and spider monkeys. Felines include pumas, ocelots and jaguars, the latter being linked to religious beliefs as the bearer of the night sun on its journey through the underworld and whose skin symbolized the power of Maya nobility.

Reptiles and amphibians also abound in the area: even today, toads and frogs are used to invoke rain. The wide range of serpents includes non-poisonous varieties such as rat snakes, Mexican vine snakes that blend in perfectly with tree branches, and enormous boas. Poisonous varieties include fer-de-lance, coral snakes and rattlesnakes. Swamp and lagoon areas are inhabited by alligators and crocodiles. Members of the insect world include horse flies, mosquitoes, bees, bumblebees, wasps, ticks, spiders, dragonflies, butterflies, moths, praying mantises and termites as well as a vast range of ants.

In this perennially green world, the Maya lived side by side with a variety of animals which they hunted for their meat and hides, subsequently used to make garments.

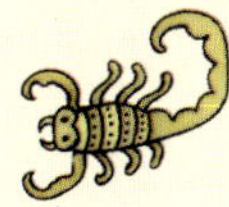     

MARINE LIFE

The Maya World's rich marine life includes crustaceans such as lobster, crab and shrimp and molluscs such as conch and oysters, and fish. The flesh and eggs of the sea turtle were eaten and its shell used as merchandise. The conch was highly prized because of the number of instruments and ornaments that could be carved from its shell. Sting ray spines used for self-sacrifice, together with the impressive pearls of the spiny oyster have been found in pre-Hispanic offerings.

REEFS

The Great Maya Reef is the second largest in the world, extending along the coast of Quintana Roo in Mexico, and Belize as far as the Gulf of Honduras. Coral is a species related to the sea anemone and grows in colonies which, after millions of years, build reefs. Brilliantly colored sponges, sea fans and algae festoon the coral formations, resembling underground gardens.

COASTLINES

The shorelines of the Maya World are variously interrupted by lagoons, bays, coves, headlands, cliffs and islands. The Maya used these geographical features as natural harbors, or modified certain areas by constructing navigable channels to link bodies of water for the first time. In marshy areas, they sometimes used conch shells to stabilize the land, building wharves to facilitate loading and unloading as well as dikes or artificial islands.

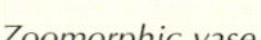

Zoomorphic vase

Battle scene, mural, Bonampak, Chiapas

SOCIAL ORGANIZATION

Nobles. Among the Maya, social hierarchy was extremely marked and the nobility enjoyed all kinds of privileges and exercised absolute power. In Yucatán, they were called *almehen,* "he who has a father and mother," reflecting an aristocratic tradition in which the idea of lineage, family filiation, and worship of one's ancestors was paramount. The nobles were the protagonists of history, as shown by the inscriptions, stelae and paintings. ***Warriors***. The paintings at Bonampak, the armed personages in sculpted monuments and clay figurines provide evidence of the presence of warriors in the Classic. During the militaristic Post-Classic, there were two types of captains *(nacom):* the governor of the provinces *(batab)* held the post while a warrior waged war. The soldiers *(holcanes)* were elected in every village. ***Artists***. Mayan art required a wide range of specialized craftsmen for its carved stone and stucco sculptures; its paintings called for skilled artists; its complicated ornaments were produced by artisans who knew how to burnish stones and shells and were familiar with the techniques for working metal. The elaborate plumes in headdresses required the patience of feather workers ***Merchants***. A sepcial class halfway between the nobility and craftsmen. ***Dancers and musicians***. Dances were an important part of religious fiestas; the Maya did not dance for pleasure. Participants were usually men, and often nobles or officials who taught the art of dance. Musicians played the *tunkul,* a small drum made out of a hollow tree trunk with a piece of deerskin stretched tightly across it. Dancers held a small drum, known as *pax,* which they beat with their hands. Wooden and clay trumpets and flutes, rattles and bone scrapers were also used. ***Working class***. Farmers, fishermen, hunters, and on the bottom rung of the ladder, slaves and prisoners.

Astronomer

Noble

Hunter

Merchant

DAILY LIFE

ECONOMIC ACTIVITIES

The common people and slaves were responsible for providing material goods through cultivation, gathering, hunting, fishing and handicrafts. Under the supervision of the priests, activities such as slash-and-burn agriculture, the hunting of large animals and building were carried out collectively. Most of the products obtained by the lower classes were handed over as tribute to the noble classes (lords and priests).

Cacao

AGRICULTURE

Mayan agriculture revolved around the cultivation of maize, beans and squash: peasants felled large trees and cleared the undergrowth which they used to fertilize the soil with ashes. They then sowed the seeds using a planting stick. After the harvest, the ground was allowed to lie fallow and the cycle repeated in an adjoining plot of land. Over time, Maya agricultural techniques evolved, since the growing population required greater productivity. In certain areas, they created terraces or raised fields and irrigation systems, and practiced crop rotation. They also cultivated cacao, avocado, zapote and ramón or breadnut.

Corn

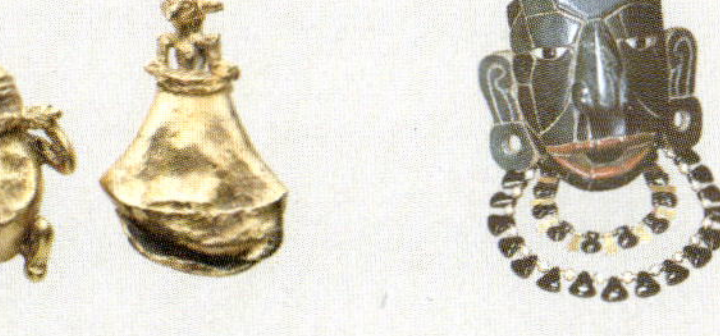

TRADE

Small-scale local trade was carried out directly between the producers whereas trade between the various regions of the Maya World and with other peoples ranging from central Mexico to Costa Rica was undertaken by professional merchants with financial possibilities and a privileged socio-political position. There were overland routes connected by *sacbeoob* (white paths in Maya) and mountain trails. Small vessels plied the coasts, stopping at villages or trade enclaves such as Cozumel.

Trade routes

- Overland routes
- Sea routes
- River routes

TRADE GOODS

Cacao
Salt
Honey

Pottery
Cotton
Obsidian

Feathers
Skins
Jade

Palenque

HUTS AND PALACES

Commoners' housing consisted of simple wooden or stone huts with palm thatch or grass roofs. The houses of the privileged classes, always located around the ceremonial center, were made out of masonry, with stone walls and vaults and stucco floors, and were usually built on terraces or platforms.

The home of a Mayan farmer

Religion

Maya gods represented the forces of nature. Each had different qualities according to his/her attributes: the same god could be celestial or terrestrial, beneficial or harmful, male or female, and provide energy for life or death. Moreover, the gods were fourfold when they supported the four corners of the earth.

The Mayan Universe

The ancient Maya represented the universe with an enormous ceiba (silk cotton tree) or *yaxché*. The branches supported the heavens (*Caan*), man's life on earth (*Cab*) took place within the trunk and the roots sank into the underworld or *Xibalba*. They believed that the earth was square and thought that it was supported by an enormous alligator or turtle. Heaven was divided into thirteen levels ruled by the same number of gods called *oxlahuntikú*, while the underworld was divided into nine levels governed by the *bolontikú*.

The earth monster or dragon was a figure of supreme energy which permeated the cosmos, and was linked to the sun, water, blood, semen and corn and depicted as various deities: Kinich Ahau, the sun, its eye; Chaac, water, its fertilizing power and Bolon Dz'acab or Ka¨wil, blood, semen and maize, its presence among men.

Sacrifice

The sacrifice was a ritual in honor of the gods. There were several types of sacrifice: self-sacrifice was an act of penitence whereby rulers, priests and nobles cut their tongues, ears and penises with blades of obsidian or manta ray spines. Human sacrifices were performed by extracting the victim's heart, and then decapitating him or shooting arrows into him. Another form was to tie a stone to the victim and throw him into a cenote.

The Mayan universe portrayed as Yaxché, the sacred ceiba tree. The universe had three levels: Caan (cielo), Cab (tierra) and Xibalbá (underworld).

Itzamná, Lord of the Gods
Moon
Ixchel, Mother of the Gods
Ek, Star
Noh Ek, Venus
Ah Yax Ak, Guardian of the Creation
Ek Chuah, God of Trade
Cuzam
Ixtab, Goddess of Suicide
Ix u na'kab Mother Earth
Charnel House
Buluc Chabtan, God of Human Sacrifice
CHAC XIB CHAC
Balam, Jaguar of the Night
Chac Xib Chac, God of Sacrifice
Ah Puch, Lord of the Underworld

MAYAN

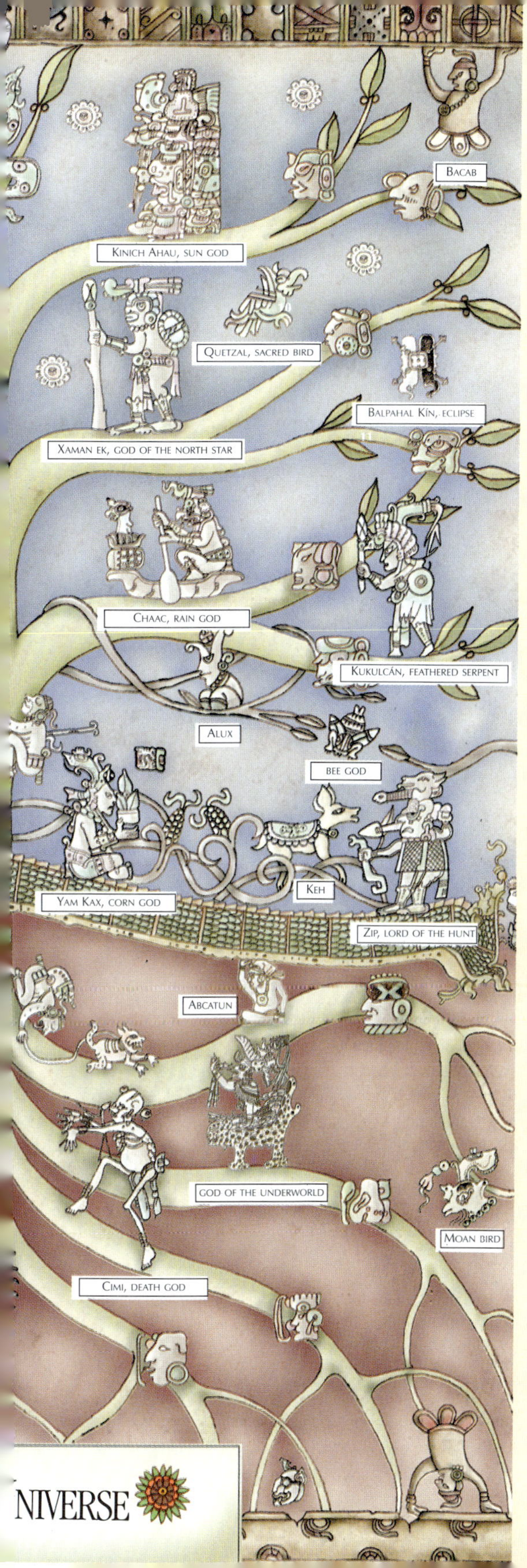

Kinich Ahau, sun god

Bacab

Quetzal, sacred bird

Balpahal Kín, eclipse

Xaman Ek, god of the North Star

Chaac, rain god

Kukulcán, feathered serpent

Alux

Bee god

Yam Kax, corn god

Keh

Zip, lord of the hunt

Abcatun

God of the underworld

Moan bird

Cimi, death god

NIVERSE

Sacred Cenote, Chichén Itzá

CENOTES AND CAVES

Cenotes or natural wells and caves were sacred places for the ancient Maya, who believed that they represented the womb of the earth and the portals to the underworld. Moreover, these cenotes were ruled by the water gods and were important places of worship. Offerings including incense, ceramics, jade and human remains have been found in these caves and wells.

Glyph and deity of the East

CARDINAL POINTS

Each cardinal point had its own tree, bird and color: North (white), South (yellow), East (red), West (black) and the center (blue), which was considered a sacred place.

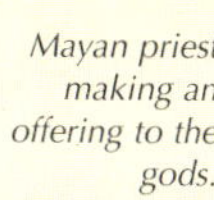

Mayan priest making an offering to the gods.

ART

The artistic achievements of the ancient Maya were the result of age-old traditions that attained a level of technological and expressive excellence to satisfy the needs of the governing elites and priests. Tools and jewelry were their worldly possessions, and are often visible in the life-size stone carvings of important personages in stelae and mural paintings.

Mayan artists were consummate painters, potters, sculptors and engravers who represented their gods, sacred animals, world view and rulers.

Monumental Mayan art is impressive not only because of its size but also because of its harmonious composition.

Murals, Bonampak, Chiapas

MURAL PAINTING

The high temperatures of the tropical forest made it difficult to work with lime. This led Mayan painters to incorporate vegetable gum into their blends of lime and coloring. This medium, known as tempera, was applied to murals with feathers and brushes.

The artistic technique used in the Bonampak murals was "dry fresco," which consists of applying a flat three to five centimeter-layer of lime mixed with a little sand to the stone. Once this layer had been polished, although while it was still fresh, figures and scenes were etched in red. After the layer had dried, the empty spaces were colored in and the initial tracings covered over. Finally, the figures were outlined in black.

COLORS

Mayan artists were forced to cope with a natural environment with few mineral resources, as a result of which they developed a tradition of making pigments that have been identified as minerals from distant lands, such as malachite and azurite, used in combination with Mayan blue to create shades of blue and green. Reds and browns were extracted from seeds, bark and clay. Purple and magenta were extracted from a sea snail and the insect called cochineal, respectively.

Mayan artists were consummate painters, potters, sculptors and engravers who represented their gods, sacred animals, world view and rulers.

USE OF COLOR

MAYAN CITIES

Mayan buildings were erected around large open squares, where the people participated in religious celebrations. Constructions made from limestone ashlars were covered with a layer of stucco that served as the base for decorating them and painting them with different colors according to their activity.

RELIEF AND DECORATION

The Maya decorated their buildings with sculptures modeled in stucco and relief carved in stone, on which they depicted their rulers ascending to power. They also portrayed the works they had commissioned during their rule, alternating them with mythical beings that consecrated the monuments

POTTERY

TECHNIQUES

Ceramics used for both domestic and ceremonial purposes were an important trade commodity. The study of Mayan ceramics (incense burners, funerary urns, figurines, plates and dishes) yields information on commercial and cultural contacts, technical and artistic changes, the tastes of the time, social classes, as well as the Mayan world view and mythology.

The painted ceramics of the Classic were made by hand, without a potter's wheel, meaning that potters began with a circular mass of clay to which they added rolled up strips of clay that they modeled until the final form was achieved. A clay base was then added, which the potters painted to achieve a bright, shiny surface. The pieces were then fired at temperatures of 800°C. Figurines were made from molds at the beginning of the Late Classic.

Incense burner, Palenque

INCENSE BURNERS AT PALENQUE

Clay incense burners were a Palenque tradition. They display a profusion of natural and fantastic images that combine to form the headdress of a deity or an ancestor to whom the piece and the incense burnt in them were dedicated.

JAINA

The clay figurines found on the island of Jaina (Campeche) are striking because of the detail in their clothes and ornamentation.

Figurines from Jaina, Campeche

Old God, Tikal, Guatemala

Polychrome plate

EXAMPLES OF CERAMICS

During the Pre-Classic, zoomorphic representations were common in ceramic objects. The adoption of polychrome decoration had its origins in the Early Classic. It is characterized by the use of red and black on a cream base, decorated with repeated geometric motifs.

The Jaina potters used two techniques to create their figurines: modeling and molding. Their realism makes them unique and they depict rulers, warriors, ball players, nobles, courtesans and weavers.

The scenes painted in the polychrome ceramics of the Late Classic have provided elements for the interpretation of Mayan culture. Polychrome pottery was used by the nobility in important rituals. Late Classic pieces reflect the degree of skill achieved by Mayan craftsmen in the handling of concept, volume and expression.

The most representative pottery of the Early Post-Classic is the so-called plumbate of the Pacific Coast. Its glaze made it a highly prized trading commodity. The introduction of thin or fine orange-type ceramics to the Yucatán Peninsula during the Post-Classic is evidence of the influence of cultures hailing from the Mexican highlands.

Vase, San Agustín Acasaguastlan, Guatemala

Classic polychrome pottery was prized by the nobility

Dresden Codex

MAYAN WRITING

THE CÓDICES

The Maya created the most complex system of pre-Hispanic writing of their time. It is based on hieroglyphs that are known to be ideographic (pictorial) but also phonetic.

The first Mayan glyphs were used to record time. These were followed by the creation of a "compound" writing system consisting basically of two types: principals, which were larger, and affixes, minor signs that could be placed around or inside the principal to form what are known as "cartridges." A series of cartridges makes a sentence which is turn is used to create texts. They usually appear in a fixed grammatical order consisting of a time marker (date), verb. subject and object, The glyph, in turn, functions in several ways, as a sign for a full stop, numeral, syllable or full word. In context, they tell the history of the leaders of each city-state.

Codices are hieroglyphic manuscripts whose "pages" are folded in the shape of a screen. They were made from tree bark or deerskin and scribes wrote on them using paintbrushes or feathers which they dipped in black or red paint. The three Mayan codices that have survived to this day are the Paris, the Madrid and the Dresden codices, currently held in these three cities respectively.

The authors of the codices were called ah ts'ib and ah woh (scribes and painters). They were priests with a knowledge of history and medicine. They also knew how to use the calendar for their ceremonies.

Glyphs used to be written in three ways: normal, head variant and full body variant.

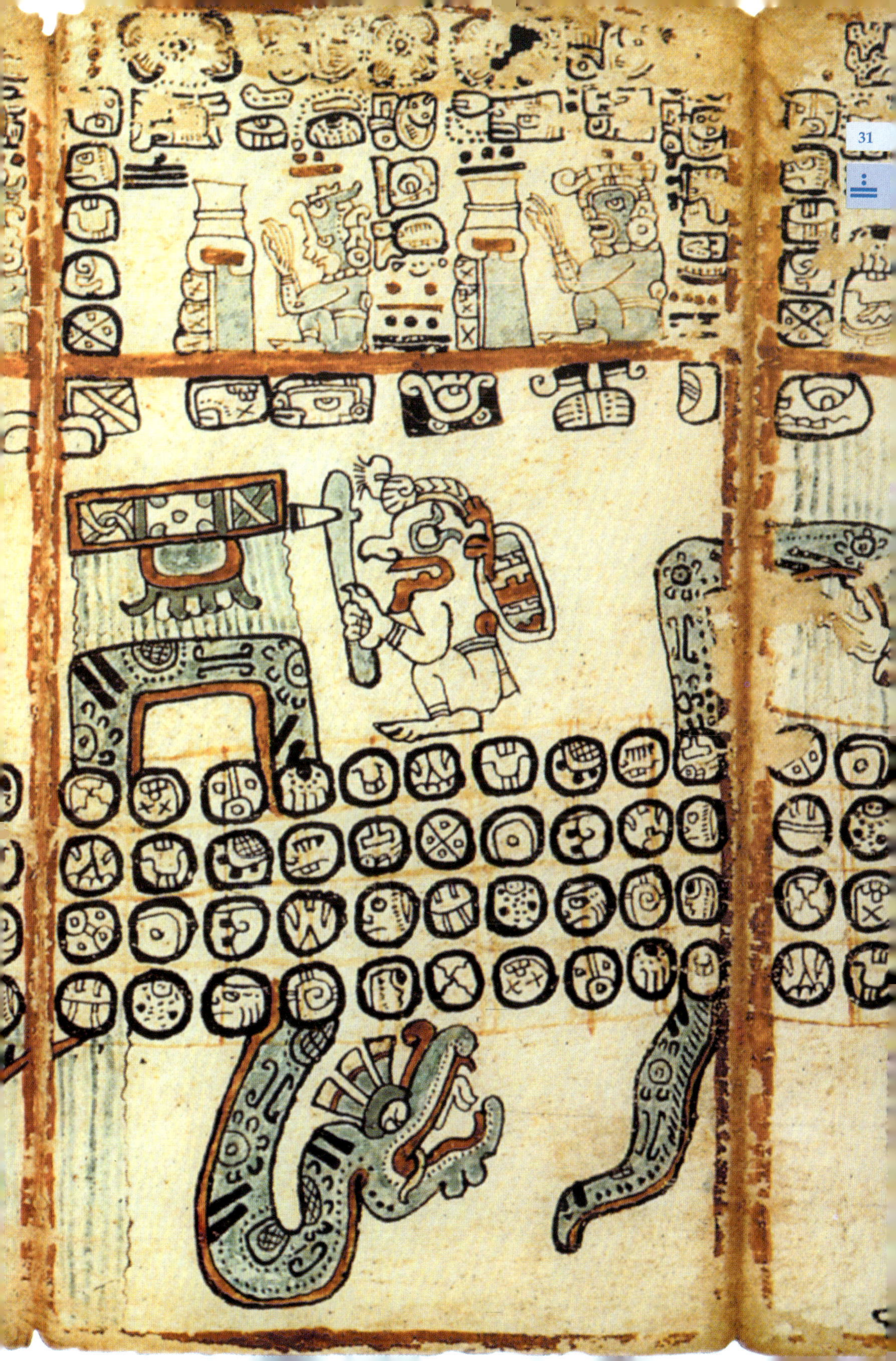

THE MAYAN CALENDAR

The Maya, who thought that time was cyclical, needed to justify the lives and work of their sovereigns, find out about agricultural and ceremonial periods and chart the courses of heavenly bodies. To this end, they established virtually perfect systems of calculating time, such as the tzolkin, a 260-day ritual calendar consisting of twelve numbers and twenty days represented by glyphs and the haab, a 365-day civil calendar or "vague year" comprising nineteen months. In fact, it consisted of eighteen twenty-day months with an interval of five unlucky days called uayeb, which preceded the new Year. These were days of misfortune when accidents could happen.

THE TZOLKÍN

1. The day bearer god
2. Numbers of the days
3. Hieroglyphics of 20 days

THE HAAB

4. Vague year of 365 days
5. Hieroglyphics of the 19 months

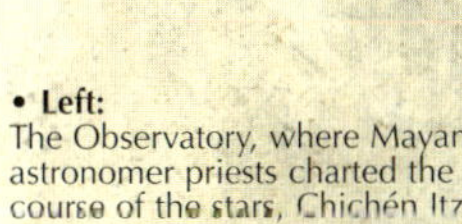

• Left:
The Observatory, where Mayan astronomer priests charted the course of the stars, Chichén Itzá

HOW DOES THE CALENDAR WORK

The period of 52 years of 365 days resulting from the combination of the tzolkin with the haab, in which each day of one cycle corresponded to a day in the other, is known as the "calendar wheel." Once the 52-year cycle had elapsed, the same date would occur, resulting in 18,9809 different combinations consisting of a day name, a number and the position of a specific month.

CONSTELLATIONS

Venus

Orion

Pleiades

Scorpio

Moon

Star

STONE SCULPTURES AND INSCRIPTIONS

CARVINGS, STUCCO & STELAE

The ancient Maya generally used limestone for their sculptures, since it was available in plentiful supply in the area and easy to work with when it had recently been extracted. The material was transported using tree trunks, raised and eventually carved. The sculptors used stone tools; flint chisels and spherical hammers. The finished effect was achieved by abrasion, culminating in an application of stucco and a layer of paint: red for buildings and sacred colors for bas-reliefs. Facades, lintels and walls were decorated with bas-reliefs representing rulers and gods, masks and animals, in addition to inscriptions and geometric features. Stucco was used to represent figures, heads and masks on buildings. Monuments such as altars, thrones and stelae proliferated in the city squares.

The practice of erecting stelae or standing began in the pre-Classic period. They represented city rulers and commemorated important events during their reign.

Stucco mask, Kohunlich, Quintana Roo

To date, lists of ruling dynasties have been re-constructed for approximately twenty Classic cities through the hieroglyphic interpretation of the stelae and inscriptions on buildings.

By the Post-Classic, the custom of building stelae had been abandoned. They were replaced by worked skulls, jaguars and eagles devouring human heads.

The Chac-mool, the Atlanteans and standard bearers built in the Toltec tradition are a fine example of monumental sculpture from the Post-Classic.

Artistic representation of the Great Plaza, sacred heart of Chichén Itzá, Yucatán

JADE

In pre-Hispanic times, jade was a sacred stone that symbolized eternity, royal breath, life, fertility and power. It could only be owned by the nobility. Specialized craftsmen were responsible for obtaining it and carving objects out of it. It could be replaced by other hard green stones and still maintain the same symbolism.

Jade masks were usually made using the mosaic technique, with pieces of shell and obsidian for the eyes and mouth. They were used as death masks for governors so that the latter would be recognized as sovereigns by the gods and treated accordingly.

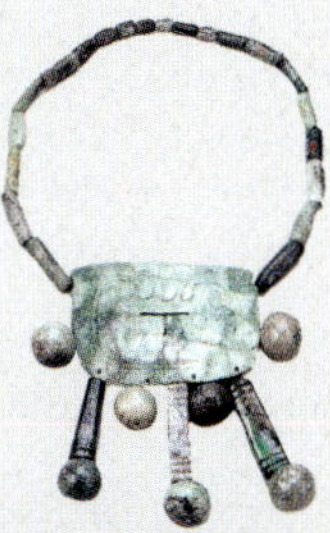

Jade necklace

Wood. Wood was used to make small sculpted objects, as well as articles for royalty. Some lintels carved in wood have survived to date.

Shell. *Spondylus* shells were used by the Maya rulers as insignias comparable to jade pectorals. Some women wore open shells over their stomachs. The Maya also made beads and pieces for mosaics. *Strombus* shells were used as trumpets.

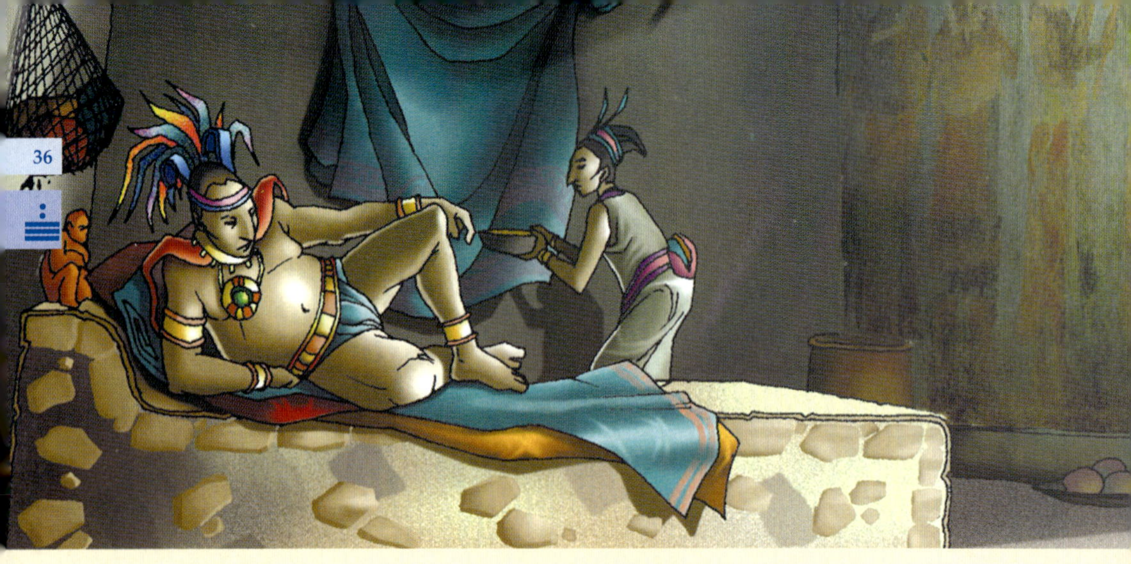

Residential quarters for the nobility

ARCHITECTURE

In Mayan architecture, nothing is fortuitous; all the details were planned beforehand, together with the proportions of each element. The basic planning unit was the straight patio, plaza or terrace, which culminated in the construction of major cities, with complex sets of stone buildings. A new structure was often superimposed over an existing one, over a long period of time, thereby channeling the sacred energy of the site into recently consecrated buildings.

Tikal

CONSTRUCCIONS

Mayan constructions ranged from very small buildings to structures of several levels. Several rooms were built on broad platforms or raised, terraced pyramids with small temples with cresting on the front, back and central walls. They generally formed part of orderly complexes, quadrangles, groups of temples or acropolises.

SUPERIMPOSED PYRAMIDS

The Maya used to construct new buildings on top of existing ones. This is why it is common to find substructures that the various stages of building in cities to be ascertained.

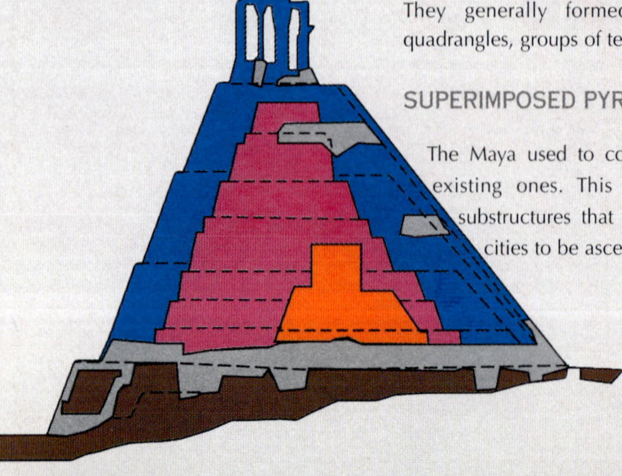

THE BALL GAME

The ball game was a constant feature of Mayan cities. During the Classic, ball courts were generally open, with low walls. By the post-Classic, they had expanded; the ends were finished off with crossbeams, and the walls were depicted with stairs and temples.

Ball player

DISTRIBUTION

The population was distributed concentrically around the ceremonial center, so that the circle closest to the latter was occupied by the nobles while those furthest away were occupied by the working class.

The poor lived in rectangular houses with rounded corners. The walls would have been made from tree trunks or stones, with plaited cane and mud or thatched palm roofs. The Maya tended to settle in areas with a plentiful water supply, usually near freshwater lagoons, rivers, cenotes or watering places.

Some temples and pyramids in the ceremonial heart of the city were erected as funeral monuments since they housed the tombs of powerful governors. When sovereigns died, they were buried with great ceremony. They took rich offerings of jade, ceramics and even slaves to wait on them during their journey to the underworld.

The Palace, Palenque, Chiapas

MEXICO

POLITICAL DIVISION

TABASCO 46

Map 1
Pomoná E3, 48, Comalcalco D1, 49, La Venta (not shown), 49, Malpasito E1, 49, Reforma E3, 49

CHIAPAS 50

Maps 1 & 2
Palenque Map 1 E2, 52, Yaxchilán Map 2 F3, 56, Bonampak Map 2 G3, 57, Izapa Map 2 H2, 58
Chinkultic Map 2 G2, 58, Tenam Puente Map 2 G2, 58, Toniná Map 2 F2, 59

CAMPECHE 60

Map 1
Xtampak C4, 62, Xtabas C4, 62
Dzibilnocac C4, 62, Hochob C4, 63, Jaina C4, 63, Río Bec D5, 64
Chicanná D5, 64, Xpuhil D5, 65
Hormiguero D4, 65, Becán D5, 65
Balamkú D4, 65, Nadzcaan D4, 66
Calakmul E4, 66, Edzná C4, 67

YUCATÁN 68

Map 1
Chichén Itzá B5, 72, Acanceh B4, 76, Dzibilchaltún A4, 77, Mayapán B4, 77, Izamal B5, 77, Balancanché B5, 77, Xcambó A5, 77, Ake B5, 77, Ek Balam B6, 77, Labná C4, 80, Xlapak C4, 80, Sayil C4, 80, Kabah B4, 82, Oxkintok B4, 82, Chacmultún C5, 82, Loltún B4, 82, Uxmal B4, 85

QUINTANA ROO 86

Map 1
Oxtankah D6, 90, Chacchobén D6, 90, Muyil C6, 91, Dzibanché D5, 91, Kohunlich D5, 92, Chakanbakán D5, 92, El Rey B7, 93, Xaman-Há B7, 93, San Gervasio B7, 93, Xel-Há B6, 94, Cobá B6, 94, Tulum C6, 97

Norte
Mundo
Simbology
Reserve
Airport
Airstip
Hotel
Gas station
Museum
Waterfalls
Toll road
Major highway
Secondary road
Dirt road
El Cuyo
Holbox
Isla Contoy
Dzonot
Colonia Yucatán
Chiquilá
Ecab
Área Protegida Yum Balam
El Meco
Puerto Juárez
Isla Mujeres
San Ángel
La Sierra
Kantunilkín
Leona Vicario
Cancún
El Rey
Yokdzonot
Xcan
Ek Balam
Central Vallarta
Puerto Morelos
Chemax
Playa del Carmen
Xcaret
Paamul
El Real
San Gervasio
Isla Cozumel
Cobá
San Juan
Akumal
Xel-Há
El Cedral
Tankah
Tulum
Madero
Muyil
Chumpón
Xlahpac
Santa Rosa
Señor
Vigía Chico
Quintana Roo
Felipe Carrillo Puerto
Reserva de la Biósfera Sian Ka'an
Nohbec
Reserva de Uaymil
El Uvero
Limones
Placer
Cafetal
Buenavista
Río Indio
Majahual
Banco Chinchorro
Xcalak
Tabasco
El Bosque
Frontera
Puerto Ceiba
Paraíso
Mirama
Chiltepec
Comalcalco
Cupilco
Jalpa
Nacajuca
Cunduacán
Jonuta
Palizada
Concepción
Villahermosa
Cárdena
Macuspana
San Pedro
Tortuguero
Teapa
Tapijulapa
Pichucalco
Villa Luz
Oxolotán
Tila
Tumbalá
Tapilula
Belice
Turneffe Islands
Mundo Maya • Arqueología

Belice
Honduras
El Salvador
Nicaragua
Belize City
Belmopan
Tegucigalpa
San Salvador
Turneffe Islands
Altun-Ha
Lamanai
Ladyville
San José
Xunantunich
Roaring Creek
San Ignacio
Society Hall Nature Reserve
Pomona
Dangriga
Benque Viejo
Cahal Pech
Melchor Mencos
Augustine
Caracol
Cockscomb Basin Wildlife Sanctuary
Seine Bight Village
Placencia
Big Creek
Medina Bank
Nim Li Punit
Lubaantun
Monkey River Town
Punta Gorda
Blue Creek
San Antonio
Pusilha
Barranco
Naachtún
Río Azul
Kinal
Xultún
La Muralla
Zacatal
El Tintal
El Zotz
Uaxactún
Tikal
Nakum
El Remate
Yaxha
Ixlú
Topoxté
Flores
El Cruce
Santa Ana
Ceibal
Ixcún
Dolores
Poptún
Naj Tunich
Machaquilá
San Luis
Modesto Méndez
Livingston
Biotopo Chocón Machacas
Puerto Barrios
Cahabón
El Estor
Quiriguá
Reserva de la Biosfera Sierra de las Minas
Río Hondo
Zacapa
Parque Nacional Cerro Azul
Quimistán
Sula
La Entrada
Florida
Chiquimula
San Luis Jilotepeque
Copán
Santa Rosa del Copán
Cucuyagua
San Pedro Pinula
Esquipulas
Nueva Ocotepeque
Metapán
La Palma
San Cristóbal
Jutiapa
Tazumal
Santa Ana
Chalatenango
Dulce Nombre de María
Tejutla
Izalco
Ahuachapán
Sonsonate
Acajutla
Joya de Cerén
San Andrés
Panchimalco
La Libertad
Costa del Sol
La Herradura
Zacatecoluca
San Vicente
San Sebastián Ilobasco
Sensuntepeque
Guatajiagua
Santiago de María
El Triunfo
Usulután
San Miguel
San Francisco Gotera
Santa Rosa de Lima
El Cuco
Puerto Cortés
Omoa
San Pedro Sula
Cofradía
El Progreso
Tela
Parque Nacional Jannete Kawas
La Masica
La Ceiba
Nueva Armenia
Jutiapa
Olan
Morazán
Jocón
Arenal
Yoro
El Negrito
Parque Nacional Pico Pijal
Santa Rita
Petoa
Trinidad
Pulahpanzak
Santa Bárbara
Parque Nacional Santa Bárbara
Parque Nacional Azul Meambar
Salitrón
Parque Nacional Celaque
Gracias
San Manuel de Colohete
San Sebastián
Siguatepeque
Comayagua
Parque Nacional Comayagua
La Esperanza
La Paz
Montañas de Comayagua
Talanga
Campamento
Juticalp
Santa Lucía
Parque Nacional La Tigra
Yuscarán
Danl
El Paraíso
Concepción
Marcala
Nueva Esparta
Santa Ana
Sabana Grande
Goascorán
Nacaome
San Lorenzo
El Espino
Choluteca
Monjarás
Cedeño
Somotillo
Chinandega
CA-1
CA-2
CA-3
CA-4
CA-5
CA-9
F
G
H
I
J
4
5
6
7

Central America

M E X

I C O

TABASCO

C H I A

P A S

• **Previous photo**
Panoramic view, Palenque

The Palace

Between 8000 and 3000 B.C., groups of hunters settled in the mountains of Chiapas, the first villages appearing between 3000 and 1000 B.C. on the Pacific Coast. The early Preclassic (300 BC – A.D. 250) saw the development of certain sites such as Chiapa de Corzo and Altamira, which gave rise to the consolidation of Maya art and architecture.

During the Classic (A.D. 250 - 900), state societies emerged in the Usumacinta river basin. In various eras, the rulers of powerful cities such as Palenque, Yaxchilán and Bonampak forged alliances, traded or fought, events that are recorded in the stone monuments of the zone.

Following the decline at the end of the Classic, the Post-Classic period of constant war continued in the Highlands of Chiapas and Guatemala, until the time of the Spanish conquest.

Temple of the Skull

Templos de Palenque

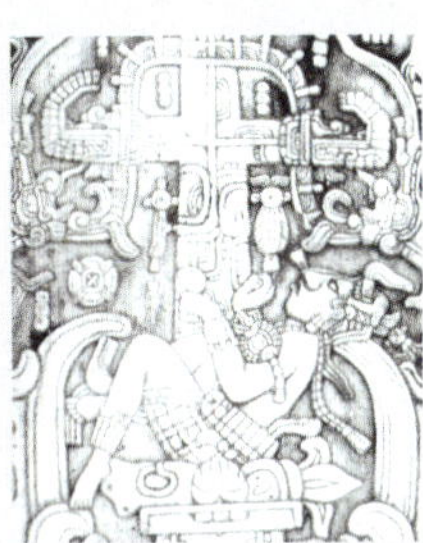
Carved tablet showing Lord Pacal

PALENQUE

Site in northern Chiapas that developed during the Late Classic when it was the capital of an extensive region. Its apogee lasted from A.D. 615 to 683, during the reign of Lord Pacal or Sun-shield. He was followed by his son Chan Bahlum or Serpent-Jaguar. Temples and buildings are distributed over a hilly area and surrounded by forest. The buildings are architecturally linked to the Palace complex, set within the largest plaza, also the site of the Temple of Inscriptions and Temple XI. Other important buildings are: Temples of the Foliated Cross, the Cross and the Sun. Pacal ruled Palenque when the city was at its peak. The carving on the lid of his sarcophagus symbolizes the Mayan cosmovision.

View of the Palace and the Temple of the Inscriptions

Palenque archaeological site

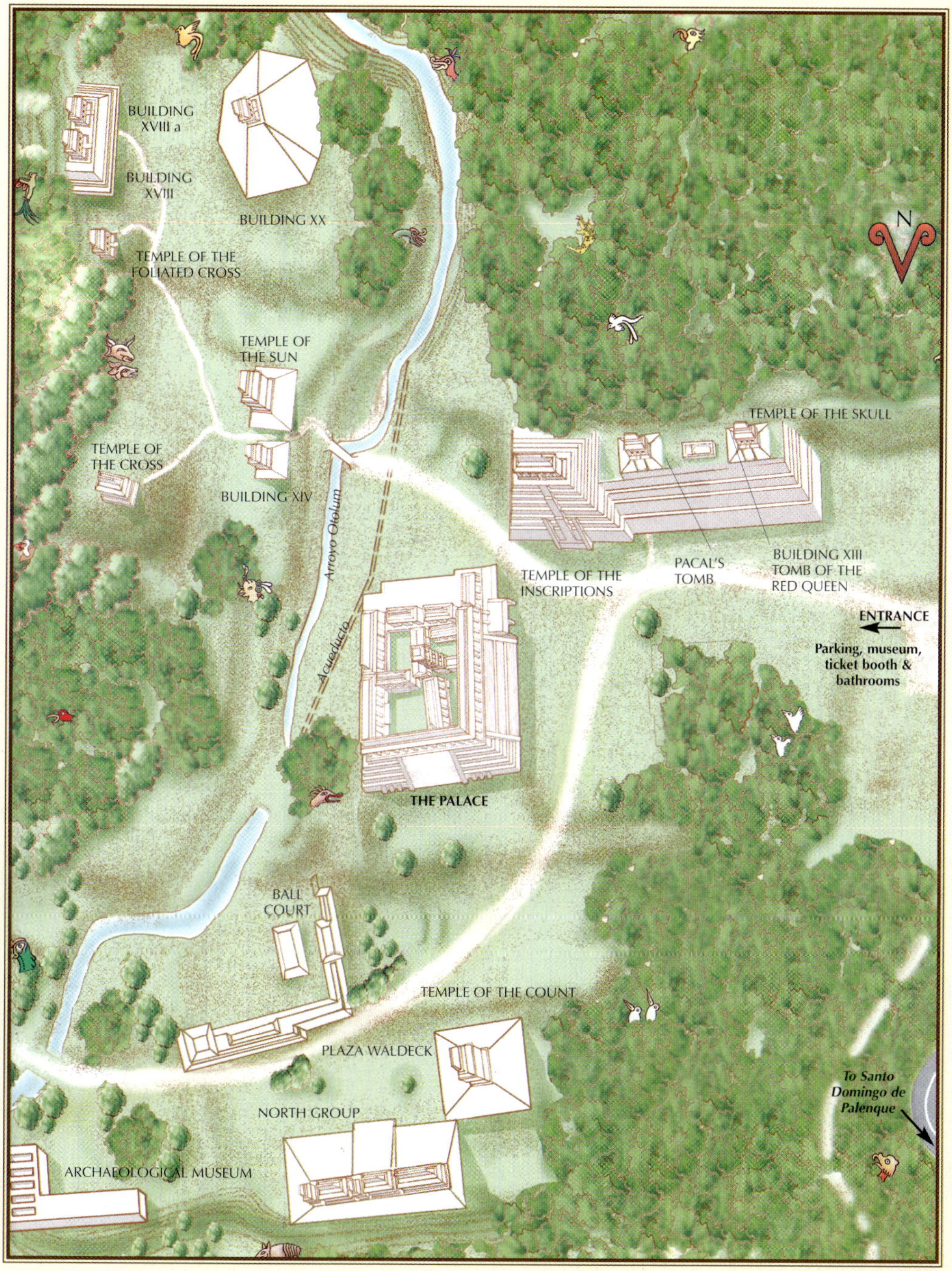

BUILDING XVIII a
BUILDING XVIII
BUILDING XX
TEMPLE OF THE FOLIATED CROSS
TEMPLE OF THE SUN
TEMPLE OF THE CROSS
BUILDING XIV
Arroyo Otolum
Acueducto
TEMPLE OF THE SKULL
TEMPLE OF THE INSCRIPTIONS
PACAL'S TOMB
BUILDING XIII TOMB OF THE RED QUEEN
ENTRANCE
Parking, museum, ticket booth & bathrooms
THE PALACE
BALL COURT
TEMPLE OF THE COUNT
PLAZA WALDECK
NORTH GROUP
ARCHAEOLOGICAL MUSEUM
To Santo Domingo de Palenque
N

Palenque's stone and modeled stucco sculpture is particularly striking. The masks, memorial tablets, bas-reliefs and hieroglyphic inscriptions in several of the buildings have provided archaeologists with valuable information on the city. The site museum boasts displays of stelae, tablets, clay figurines, pottery, and jade, shell and obsidian artifacts.

• **Left:**
Illustration of the Palace, Palenque, by Frederick Catherwood

BUILDINGS IN PALENQUE

The Palace: A labyrinth of rooms and walkways, the Palace is Palenque's most complex building and was modified several times during its history. A tower rises from the center of the grouping.

Temple of the Inscriptions: The most famous building on the site, this striking white temple owes its name to the three panels of hieroglyphic inscriptions in the upper sanctuary. Site of Pacal's tomb.

Temple of the Skull: Also known as Temple XII, it stands on a platform to the west of the Temple of Inscriptions. The most striking aspect of the temple is the stucco relief of a human skull.

Temple of the Cross: The Panel of the Cross (now in the National Anthropology Museum) once decorated the shrine that crowned the temple. The two side carvings can still be seen in the sanctuary.

Temple of the Sun: Temple erected on a pyramid base and crowned by a finely-detailed roof crest. Carved from limestone, the Sun Panel is an artistic masterpiece.

Temple of the Foliated Cross: Stands on a pyramid still covered with vegetation. The panel that gives the building its name depicts corn sprouting from the ground in the shape of a cross.

Northern Group: Grouping of five temples which show the ingenious way the Maya adapted their buildings to take account of the uneven terrain.

Temple of the Cross

Temple of the Sun

Temple of the Count

Temple of the Inscriptions

YAXCHILÁN

Set in the Lacandon rainforest, Yaxchilán (A.D. 250-900) has around 120 buildings in its central area, distributed between three main complexes; the Great Plaza, parallel to the Usumacinta River and the Great Acropolis and the Small Acropolis, both adapted through terraces and platforms to the low hills that rise to the south of the Great Square. The three squares are linked by staircases, ramps and distribution terraces.

The architecture of the city is characterized by stelae, lintels, altars and stairs, as well as by reliefs modeled in stucco and mural painting.

Shield Jaguar I, the queen of Shield Jaguar I, Bird Jaguar IV, Shield Jaguar II and Skull III ruled consecutively from A.D. 681 to 800.

Hieroglyphic inscriptions have shed light on part of the history of the area:

During the period when Shield Jaguar I ruled (A.D. 681-742), the city consolidated its military supremacy.

On the death of Shield Jaguar 1, one of his wives apparently assumed power for a brief period (A.D. 742 to 752) during which she prepared her son, Bird Jaguar IV (A.D. 752-768) for his accession to the throne.

Yaxchilán

Bonampak

BONAMPAK

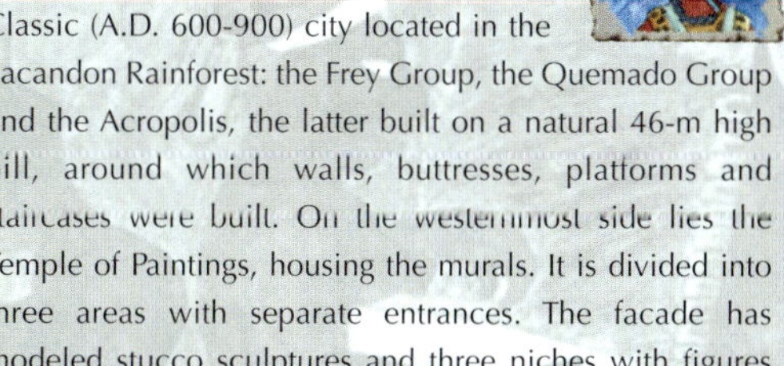

Three complexes comprise this Late Classic (A.D. 600-900) city located in the Lacandon Rainforest: the Frey Group, the Quemado Group and the Acropolis, the latter built on a natural 46-m high hill, around which walls, buttresses, platforms and staircases were built. On the westernmost side lies the Temple of Paintings, housing the murals. It is divided into three areas with separate entrances. The facade has modeled stucco sculptures and three niches with figures seated on thrones. In addition to paintings, Bonampak boasts lintels, friezes and exquisitely beautiful stelae.

Broadly speaking, the murals narrate a history that begins with the presentation of a small child at the royal court of King Chaan Muan (Sky-Bird-Muan), an event celebrated with musicians. Immediately afterwards, they engage in a battle during which prisoners are taken for sacrifice.

Room two represents Chaan Muan at the top of a staircase, while opposite him a person is depicted pleading for mercy and another prisoner lies at his feet. The hands of the defeated men are bleeding because of the punishment inflicted on them.

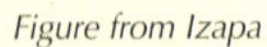

Figure from Izapa

Figure from Izapa

IZAPA

Founded around 1500 B.C., this was the largest civic and religious site on the Pacific plain for a thousand years. It initially comprised over 160 buildings, including pyramids and platforms, distributed around the squares. Opposite the buildings stand 252 stone monuments, most of which are carved, and 89 engraved stelae, at the foot of which there are usually stone altars. The scenes engraved on the monuments help one to understand what life must have been like in this ancient city.

Acropolis, Chinkultic

CHINKULTIC

The occupation of Chinkultic ("terraced well") lasted for several years, but the city reached its architectural peak during the Late Classic (A.D. 600-900). The earliest mention of the site is made by Eduard Seler, who visited it in the late 19th century. Studies on pottery excavated in the area have enabled archaeologists to reconstruct its chronology. The housing area consists of nearly two hundred mounds grouped into six main complexes including the Acropolis or Group A, the Group B quadrangle and Group C, with the ballcourt and large platform.

TENAM PUENTE

Site which developed during the Classic and post-Classic periods. Located on a hill which was terraced in order to erect buildings, squares and ball games, it occupies an area of approximately two square kilometers, containing civil and religious buildings, together with others used for housing. It is built on large platforms with monumental retaining walls (*Tenam* means "fortification" in Náhuatl). Major buildings include the Acropolis, with structures 4 and 7 and its three ballcourts.

The Chinkultic Disc, Chiapas. Portrays a ball player.

TONINÁ

Ceremonial city of the Late Classic (A.D. 600-900) a short distance from Ocosingo. The Acropolis, built on a natural elevation, at the basis of which lies a large plaza, with a ball court, several temples, altars and stelae, consists of seven platforms. The Palace of the Underworld is on the third, and the Palace of the Grecian Frets and War on the fourth. The sixth contains the Mural of the Four Suns, a sort of stucco codex depicting the four cosmognonic eras. The Temples of the Prisoners and the Smoking Mirror stand on the seventh platform. At the foot of the staircase of this platform stands a sculpture of Tzotz Choj, the last ruler of Toniná.

Toniná was a warlike city and its friezes depict the struggle between life and death, the sun and periods of time. Captives, presumably from rival cities, are shown before and after being sacrificed, during the decapitation ritual.

C A M P

E C H E

• **Previous photo:**
Nuns' Quadrangle, Uxmal

Puuc Route

Uxmal • Labná • Xlapak • Sayil • Kabah • Oxkintok • Chacmultún • Loltún

Chaac, Rain god

To the west of the Yucatán lie several cities nestled in a low range of hills called Puuc (in Maya, *puuc* means "hill"), all of which flourished during the Late Classic (A.D. 600-1000). Common features of these World Heritage Site cities include the use of "concrete" covered with intricately carved stones and buildings erected on rectangular bases. Although the lower surfaces are rarely decorated, the upper surfaces display elaborate mosaic-like geometrical sculptures, including long-nosed masks above the doors and in the corners, small drums, spikes, latticework and niches.

Labná

This site has a residential palace of various levels whose frieze is decorated with symbolic and geometric elements. One of the corners has a serpent's head out of whose jaws a man's head emerges. The Palace is linked to the south by means of a *sacbé* that crosses the main square, ending in a pyramidal base topped with a temple near the Monumental Arch.

Each side of the Arch is decorated with cornices with geometric elements in the shape of undulating snakes surrounded by lattice work; impressive masks of the god Chaac are displayed at either end.

Xlapak

This site was probably ruled by Uxmal. The best known construction is the Palace, a single-storey building with nine rooms whose upper facade is decorated with frets, small columns and three rows of Chaac masks.

Sayil

One of the most prominent buildings in Sayil is the Great Palace, a monumental, three-storey structure containing 94 rooms divided by columns. The latter include columns with capitals, small columns and friezes with masks and gods. A *sacbé* connects the complex to the two-storey South Palace, the ball court and a platform with carved stelae. Halfway along the *sacbé* stands El Mirador, a building associated with the ancient elite.

The Palace, Sayil

Arch of Labná

Left, the Palace of the Governor, Uxmal

Uxmal

Although Uxmal was first settled in 800 B.C., the most characteristic and beautiful Puuc buildings were built at the time when Uxmal ("thrice built" in Maya) was the major political capital in southwestern Yucatán, during the Classic period (A.D. 200-950). The richly carved upper facades were assembled using hundreds of different elements to create a sort of stone mosaic that incorporated complex motifs and symbolic elements.

To solve the problem of water shortages in the Puuc hills, the Maya collected rainwater using canals and *chultunes* (water deposits), thereby guaranteeing agricultural production during the dry season.

During the Post-Classic, the arrival of the Xiu marked a change in the ceremonial center. This new group seized power and the control of trading activities and tribute through a network of alliances, thereby consolidating its regional hegemony.

The western side of Temple IV, crowning the Pyramid of the Magician resembles an enormous zoomorphic mask, and features elements of the architectural style from the Chenes region, in neighboring Campeche.

The different building levels of the Nuns' Quadrangle feature a variety of decorative elements. The central motif of the eastern frieze is an elderly ruler with an elaborate feather headdress.

The succession of carved frets and Chaac masks creates the illusion of a serpent slithering across the eastern frieze of the Governor's Palace.

Other important buildings are El Palomar or the Dovecote, the Great Pyramid, the House of the Turtle, the Cemetery, the Quadrangle of the Birds and the Ball Court.

Nuns' Quadrangle

Palace of the Governor

QUINTA

N A   R O O

Oxtankah

Plaza, Dzibanché

Muyil

- **Previous photos**
1. Temple of the Wind, Tulum
2. Pyramid of Nohoch Mul, Cobá
3. Acropolis, Kinichná

Virtually all the important archaeological sites in Quintana Roo have their origins in the pre-Classic, despite the fact that no significant groups of constructions have survived from this period. The influence of Teotihuacan was felt during the Early Classic, while the Río Bec style, with El Petén elements, proliferated during the Late Classic in the south of the state. Following the collapse of Mayapán (Late Post-Classic) the Yucatán peninsula was divided into a series of chiefdoms, of which Ecab, Cochuah, Uaymil and Chactemal were located in what is now the state of Quintana Roo, on the shores of which the East Coast architectural style developed.

OXTANKAH

Oxtankah ("three districts") was the result of a lengthy construction process. Some of its earliest buildings, erected between 200 and 600 B.C., can still be seen in the Bee and Column Plazas. During the 15th and 16th centuries, Maya groups re-inhabited the city, using stone from the dilapidated old buildings to build houses, walls and small temples, remains of which are still extant.

CHACCHOBEN

Meaning "red maize" in Maya, Chacchoben is one of the most important settlements to the north of the Bacalar lagoon. To date, Temples 1 and 2, dating from the Early Classic, have been restored, together with a building dated to between the Early and Late Classic, in which a bench decorated with mural painting displaying ceremonial motifs was found. The building style is Petén, which characterized the south of Quintana Roo during this period.

Dzibanché

MUYIL

A jungle track links the principal vestiges of Muyil, which include the bases of several pyramids and a number of platforms. The most striking construction is a 15-m high pyramidal base with the remains of staircases and a temple with a roof comb. A post-Classic temple stands on the shores of the Muyil lagoon.

DZIBANCHÉ

This site, which reached its apogee between A.D. 300 and 1200, was discovered by Thomas Gann in 1927 and called *Dzibanché* ("writing on wood" in Maya) because of the calendar symbols found in Temple VI or the Temple of Lintels. Temples I and II are particularly outstanding. A tomb with sumptuous offerings was found in the former, including a pot with a figure of an owl on the lid, which is why the building is known as the Temple of the Owl. Other buildings include the Temple of the Cormorants and the North and South plazas that form the Xibalbá Patio and Gann Square, which contains Building XIII or the Building of the Captives.

KOHUNLICH

Kohunlich (from the English words *cohune* and ridge: "ridge of cohune palms") was reported in 1912 as *Clarksville* by Raymond Merwin. In the mid-1960s, Víctor Segovia excavated the site and unearthed the first stage of construction associated with El Petén, evident in the Building of the Masks, the staircase of which is flanked by eight stucco masks representing the sun god, Kinich Ahau. The second stage is the Río Bec style, as seen in the sub-structure of the Acropolis. A third stage is reflected in modest buildings.

The Kohunlich masks combine human features (rulers) with mythical elements: enormous eyes linked to Kinich Ahau (Lord Sun Face), and jade earflaps complemented with celestial serpents. Jaguar figures appear above and below the faces: the lower one symbolizes the nocturnal sun in his journey through the underworld, while the upper one is linked to the diurnal sun.

CHAKANBAKÁN

Chakanbakán ("Surrounded by savanna") in Maya, is located near Caoba and the border with Campeche. Its importance lies in its antiquity and the fact that it has one of the largest buildings with masks in the Maya World. According to specialists, the construction called Nohoch Balam was built between 300 and 50 B.C. Scholars believe that the masks represent deities associated with the jaguar, the sacred animal of the ancient Maya.

Mask, Kohunlich

Chakanbakán

El Rey

The site owes its name to the stucco figure with a human face found in one of the buildings and now on display at the Archaeological Museum in Cancún. The site (300 B.C. - A.D. 1500) comprises two squares surrounded by East Coast-style buildings, where several graves without offerings have been found. El Rey belonged to the chiefdom of Ecab and formed part of the network of sites that engaged in coastal trade. Its inhabitants earned their livelihood from fishing, salt, honey and incense.

El Rey

Xaman-Há

The name of this post-Classic site means "water from the North". It was here that pilgrims made the crossing to Cozumel to worship at the shrines of the goddess Ixchel. Some of the site's buildings exemplify the East Coast style, and can be seen on the grounds of the Playacar residential area.

San Gervasio

Cozumel (*Cuzamil:* "place of swallows") was an important tradie center that attracted Maya merchants from as far away from Honduras who came to ply their wares and worship the goddess Ixchel. The site of San Gervasio consists of six architectural groups dating from two different periods: Early Classic and post-Classic. It comprises civic, religious and residential buildings, where several tombs have been found.

San Gervasio

AMÉRICA

CENTRAL

BELIZE

• **Previous photos**
Left: Lamanai
Right: Caracol

Belize

The first Maya-speaking group in Belize came from the Guatemalan highlands and settled in places such as Cuello, the oldest pre-Classic site (2500 B.C.) in the Maya area. The discovery of shells from the Caribbean and Guatemalan obsidian and jade corresponding to the Middle Preclassic (900-300 B.C.) proves the existence of long-distance trade. States emerged in Lamanai and Cerros which became a prosperous trading port during the late Preclassic (300 B.C. to A.D. 250). Caracol consolidated its position as the major city in the Classic when it conquered the powerful city-state of Tikal. With the invasion of Náhuatl people during the Post-Classic and the fragmentation of the northern empire, Ts'ul Uinicoob became the capital of the chiefdom of Chactemal

Santa Rita

In the early 20th century, a local doctor discovered friezes from the late Classic in Santa Rita, together with stucco murals and various tombs. Remains of ceramics from 2000 B.C., a 4th century A.D. tomb (with a skeleton and jade offerings) and a late post-Classic tomb indicate that it was occupied throughout the Maya period. Evidence shows that it was a major trade center. Much of Santa Rita is covered by what is now Corozal.

Jade, sacred stone and symbol of eternity , life, fertility and kingly power

Cerros

During the pre-Classic (around 400 B.C.) Cerros was already a trade center. From 50 B.C. onwards, construction began. One of the most important buildings is Structure 5, topped by a temple with gigantic masks featuring planet Venus, the morning and evening stars, and a sunrise and sunset on the south facade. The complex, with a moat and ballcourt, was unearthed during the 1970s. It was one of the earliest Maya settlements to adopt the concept of royalty, and was governed by an *ahau* or sovereign. Part of Cerros now lies under Chetumal Bay and can only be reached by boat from Corozal in the north of Belize.

Jade head, Altun Há

Xunantunich

XUNANTUNICH

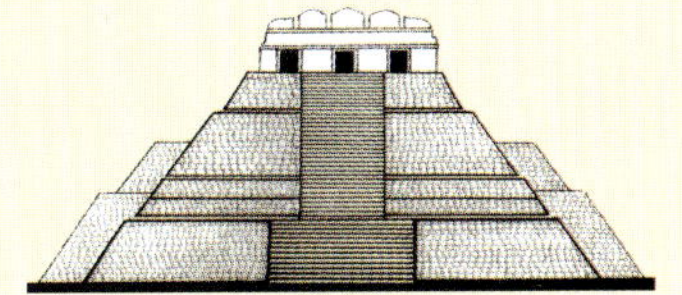

Around A.D. 900, Xunantunich ("stone maiden" in Maya) was destroyed by an earthquake and subsequently abandoned. Although excavations began in 1938, only a few buildings have been studied. There are two major plazas: A-1 and A-2, the latter dominated by Structure A-6 or El Castillo, 132 feet high, and famous for its frieze. Other important buildings include Structure A-16 or the House of the Stela, so-called because of the carved stone found there, and Structure 15.

ALTUN HÁ

Altún Ha ("stone water" in Maya) was founded around 600 B.C. and 400 years later, was trading with cities in central Mexico and others in the Maya World. The last buildings from this early stage date from A.D. 150, but others are from the Late Classic. The principal buildings include the Temple of the Green Tomb, actually a series of superimposed temples with abundant offerings, and the Temple of Stone Altars. In 1968, excavations of a tomb yielded what is still the largest jade piece excavated in the Maya area: a head of Kinich Ahau, the Sun God, weighing over nine pounds.

Altun Há at night

Cahal Pech

Cahal Pech

LUBAANTÚN

Lubaantún ("fallen stones" in Maya) was a commercial enclave, as attested by the jade, obsidian, shell and turquoise objects from other regions found there. It flourished in the late 8th century, but was abandoned shortly afterwards. It is interesting because of the building technique used: stones were simply placed one on top of another, without mortar. The largest building is only 40 feet high, but on clear days, it is possible to see Punta Gorda, 26 miles south, from the top.

CAHAL PECH

This small site, meaning "place of ticks" in Maya, is located approximately two miles outside San Ignacio, west of Belize. It was occupied in A.D. 200 and flourished during the Classic.

Nim Li Punit

CUELLO

This site was continuously occupied for at least 3,000 years until about the fifth century A.D. Nowadays, little can be seen except grassy mounds on this area of private property (ask the caretaker for permission to enter), four miles west of Orange Walk in the north of Belize. Fragments of a previously unknown style of pottery were discovered here, together with tombs where pottery vessels were placed on the heads of the dead.

* For visits ask the caretaker for permission to enter.

Caracol

Inhabited since 300 B.C., it reached its peak in A.D. 562, when it defeated Tikal in battle, thereby dominating Belize and northern Guatemala for a century. Stelae, altars and markers with glyphs commemorating dates, sovereigns and events have been found here. Its temples, pyramids, dwellings, ballcourts and plazas are linked by *sacbes*. Major constructions include the South Acropolis, Plaza A, the Temple of the Wooden Lintel and the Caana ("Heavenly Palace") which, at nearly 140 feet, is the tallest pyramid in Belize.

Lamanai

Although by the year 1500 B.C., Lamanai ("submerged crocodile" in Maya) was already inhabited, its buildings date from between 800 and 600 B.C. Structure N10-43 was constructed when the site was at its peak (late pre-Classic and early Classic). An earlier pyramid was found in the interior of Building P9-56, famous for its 13-foot-high stone mask (see left), an example of the Mayan tradition of building temples on land hallowed by their predecessors. The majority of the site's 700 buildings have yet to be excavated and are covered with dense undergrowth.

At its apogee, the city had a population of 50,000 inhabitants.

Lamanai was still inhabited during the Spanish conquest. Its inhabitants rebelled against Spanish rule and burnt two churches in the village of Indian Church.

G U A T E

M A L A

Between 1000 and 500 B.C., a sharp population increase led to the construction of large buildings in Nakbé and Tikal, in the Petén lowlands, and in Kaminaljuyú (the site of Guatemala City) and El Portón in the highlands, together with the first stelae. Kaminaljuyú controlled the obsidian trade and various trading routes in the Pacific. However, during the Late pre-Classic, these centers began to decline. As a result, Tikal consolidated its position as the political and economic center until the Classic through wars and alliances with other cities such as Calakmul. After the collapse of major centers at the end of the Classic, cities in the Highlands flourished during the Post-Classic. Various regional centers that emerged at the end of the middle phase, such as Utatlán, the capital of the Quiché Maya and Iximché, the capital of the Cakchiquel Maya, acquired greater power and importance.

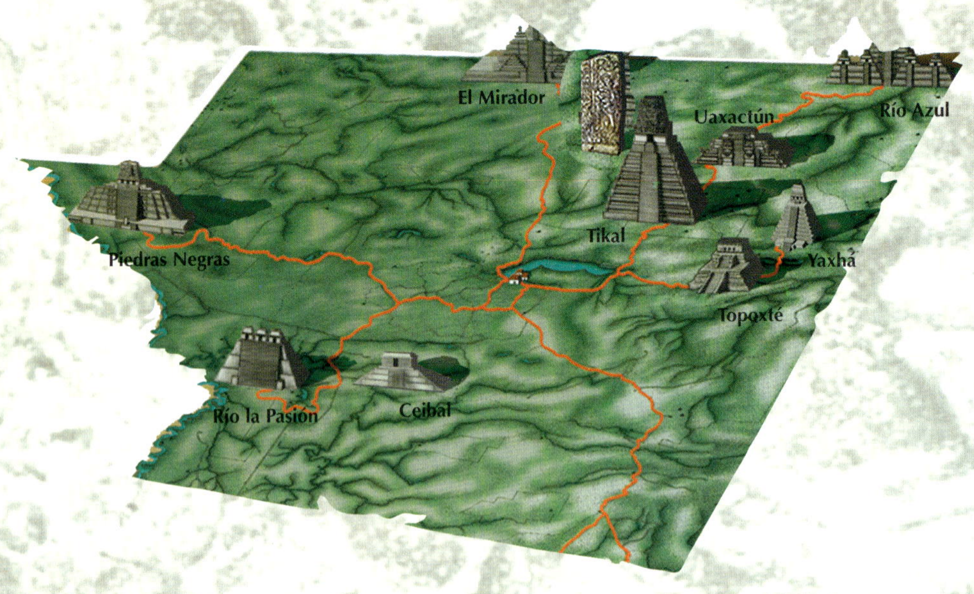

THE PETÉN

Human presence in the region dates back to prehistoric times, and major urban and ceremonial centers already existed by 200 B.C. The Maya reached their peak between A.D. 200 and 900, when they declined for reasons unknown. Many of the major sites were abandoned; others, however, lasted until the 17th century. In the early 13th century, a group of Itzá Maya from northern Yucatán settled in the Lake Petén Itzá region. Cortés came into contact with them on his way to Honduras in 1525. His chroniclers mention abandoned cities and speak of magnificent buildings. During the 19th century, logging brought the ancient centers to light.

Uaxactún

The name of this site, dating from the Middle pre-Classic, means "eight stones." It developed during the Classic and was abandoned at the beginning of the post-Classic. In A.D. 378, it was overrrun by warriors from Tikal. The royal family was executed and buried in Structure 8-VIII and Smoking Frog occupied the throne, as recorded in Stela 5 (A.D. 387). Group E, its most important building, was an observatory. The distribution of its structures is intriguing; E-1, in the north, is aligned with the summer solstice; E-II, in the center, with the spring and autumn equinoxes while E-III, in the south, is aligned with the winter solstice.

Uaxactún

Yaxhá

This site is located on the shores of the lake of the same name, 18 miles southeast of Tikal, in the Maya Biosphere Reserve. Its glyph emblem has been phonetically deciphered as *yaxha,* meaning "unchanged over time." The nucleus consists of about 500 buildings and 40 stelae, two ballcourts, at least nine pyramids higher than Temple II at Tikal and an impressive network of *sacbes.* Temple 216, in the East Acropolis, offers a panoramic view of the surroundings. Plaza C contains the only group of twin pyramids outside Tikal.

Stela, Yaxhá

Topoxté

This archaeological site is located on the southern tip of Topoxté Island, in the middle of Lake Yaxhá. It dates from the post-Classic and features two pyramids and a temple. The altars and stelae at the foot of the pyramids contain peculiar circles. This is the only island city with restored post-Classic architecture. Since 1989, Guatemala's Institute of Anthropology and History has worked extensively in Yaxhá and Topoxté.

Topoxté

Ceibal

This site, ("place of ceiba trees" in Maya) was founded by the Maya-Putún, a group from the coast of the Gulf of Mexico which dominated trade in the region. It reached its peak around A.D. 830 and was abandoned after A.D. 900. Excavation work, begun in 1960, has brought to light some of its buildings, foremost among which is Group A which has two plazas, fifteen stelae and a ballcourt. In the center of the South plaza stands Structure A-3 together with five stelae dating from A.D. 849.

Ceibal

A group of Itzá Maya from northern Yucatán settled in the area of Lake Petén Itzá

Temple I, Tikal

TIKAL

This is the largest archaeological site in the central lowlands and one of the most important in the Maya World. Its enormous dimensions are the result of nearly 2000 years (800 B.C. to A.D. 900) of continuous occupation. At its peak it covered approximately 50 square miles and supported a population of nearly 100,000 inhabitants. It was the first political entity in the Classic and dominated lesser settlements in the area. It was a great center of artisans and artists and the principal lithium producer of the time. Its scholars were well versed in the mysteries of measuring time and the movement of the stars. In 1979, Tikal was declared a World Heritage Site by UNESCO.

The Great Plaza lies at the heart of the city. This is the site of Temples I and II and the Northern and Central Acropolises. Seventy stelae and altars line the plaza and the terrace. The courtyard is coated with stucco; the first floor was built in approximately 150 B.C. while the last was completed in about A.D. 700.

Temple I

Also called the Temple of the Giant Jaguar, it stands 155 feet high. The Sanctuary of Ah Cacau is the first funerary pyramid outside the Northern Acropolis. It is crowned by a roof comb with a panel featuring the dead ruler. His grave (Tomb 116) which, at the time of its discovery, contained rich offerings, lies underneath the pyramid, inscribed with a date corresponding to A.D. 700.

Temple II

Due to its elaborate facade, this temple is also known as the Temple of the Masks. It was built in approximately A.D. 700 and is 125 feet high. One of the sculptures on the roof comb panel is thought to portray the wife of Ah Cacau.

Tikal

Central Plaza

Temple I

Temple II

Lost World , roof crests

North Acropolis

Lost World Complex

A complex of 38 buildings. The Great Pyramid (Structure 5C-54) was an observatory and was the first of its kind in the Maya World. A hundred feet tall, it has stairs on all four sides but no upper temple. In several tombs, skeletons have been found, one of which was apparently a governor during an early period. Sacrificial victims have also been discovered in Structure 5D-86.

Plaza of the Seven Temples

In addition to the seven temples of the Late Classic laid out in a row, this site contains the only triple ballcourt in Mesoamerica. The moldings of the central temple are intriguing; the altar and stela are flat, while the outer edges of Structure 5D-91 feature the sculptures of human heads.

West Plaza

The most striking feature of this Plaza is a tomb found under an unfinished building (Structure 5D-11) on the west side of the plaza. Excavations of Tomb 77 yielded ceramic objects and jade ornaments from the Late Classic in good condition. The plaza also contains altars and stelae, mostly from the Late Classic. Stela 15 is the only Early Classic Monument.

East Plaza

Early Classic group located behind Temple I, at the intersection between Maler Avenue and Méndez Avenue. The stucco floor contains one of the city's five ballcourts and was once the site of the crowded central market (Structures 5E 32 to 36).

Map of Tikal

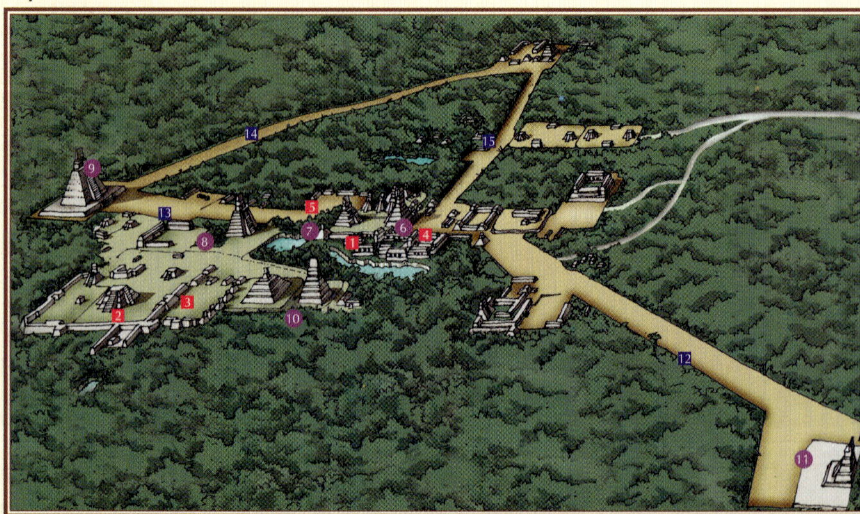

PLAZAS

1 GREAT PLAZA
2 LOST WORLD
3 SEVEN TEMPLES
4 EAST PLAZA
5 WEST PLAZA

TEMPLES

6 TEMPLE I
7 TEMPLE II
8 TEMPLE III
9 TEMPLE IV
10 TEMPLE V
11 TEMPLE VI

CAUSEWAYS

12 MÉNDEZ
13 TOZZER
14 MAUDSLAY
15 MALER

Causeways

Ancient *sacbes* or avenues leading to various buildings and complexes in the city spread out from the Great Plaza in a fan shape, along which tours of the site are conducted. All the avenues except one are named after the early explorers: Méndez, Maler, Tozzer and Maudslay.

North Acropolis

This was the burial place for the rulers of Tikal for 500 years. The oldest grave discovered to date is Tomb 22 (late 4th century) and archaeologists believe it may be that of Lord Great Jaguar Paw. Tombs 166 and 167 (Late pre-Classic) contain mural paintings and iconography. The most impressive building is Structure 5D-33, the tomb of Lord Stormy Sky.

Central Acropolis

Complex consisting of 45 buildings, mostly from the Late Classic, and six courtyards. Located south of the great plaza, it is thought to have been a residential area. The various sections, dating from different periods, contain passageways, stairways, patios and terraces. Several features indicate a life of luxury and attempts to ensure privacy.

Certain features suggest that these were the royal palaces. One of the most striking constructions is Maler's Palace (Structure 5D-65) in Courtyard 2. Courtyard 3 is surrounded by buildings with curved beams forming an elongated vault. In Courtyard 4, the original frieze of Structure 5D-49 can still be seen on the east and north walls. Courtyard 6 has larger, open spaces, together with an imposing architectural style. Structures 5D-128, 5D-53 and 5D-46 display unusual details. Graffiti figures on a vessel, together with jade, pyrite shell and obsidian objects were found under the west staircase of the latter.

South Acropolis

Its most outstanding feature is the enormous, 80-foot-high north-facing pyramid, with four palaces surrounding a central temple at the top. The acropolis has yet to be excavated and shows what the city must have looked like when the first explorers arrived.

Temple II, Tikal

Mayan vault, Tika

G Group

After the Central Acropolis, this is the complex with most buildings in the Tikal Palace style. It belongs to the Late Classic and constitutes an elongated complex with this type of buildings. It is located at the intersection between the main avenue and Méndez causeway. Access to the first courtyard on the right of the path is gained by crossing a palace with 29 rooms. At the entrance stands a gigantic stucco mask depicting a monster from Mayan mythology (Structure 5E-58).

Temple III

This is the most recent pyramid from the Late Classic in Tikal. Standing 180 feet tall and dating from A.D. 819, it may have been the tomb of Chitam (Sovereign C), the last identified ruler. It is also known as the Temple of the Jaguar Priest.

Palace of the Bat

Located just beyond Temple III, to the left. The layout of Structure 5C-13 is similar to that of the Maler Palace in the Central Acropolis. The sloping vaults and graffiti that form part of this building are of particular interest.

Temple IV

Also known as the Temple of the Two-headed Snake, this 210-foot-high temple towers above the jungle and is the tallest pre-Hispanic building in the Maya World. The lintel was taken to Switzerland by Bernoulli in 1877 and has the date A.D. 741 inscribed on it. This is a massive construction; the walls of the temple at the top are 33 feet thick.

Temple VI

Temple V

This 188-foot-high pyramid, the second tallest in Tikal, dates from A.D. 700 or 750. It is north-facing and was apparently the tomb of an unidentified ruler. It has rounded corners and modillions (ornamental brackets) the length of its staircase, but no altar or stelae. The temple at the top contains a room that is three feet wide, with ten-foot-thick walls, it is crowned by a roof comb.

Twin Pyramids

Tikal is the only city with twin pyramid complexes, the first of which was built from a scale model. This is the earliest example of pyramidal sub-structures of multiple terraces with complicated recesses and moldings that change level with each successive terrace, creating an intriguing play of light and shadow. This type of buildings is found in the N, O, P, Q and R complexes.

Twin temples, Complex Q

North Acropolis

Museums

The Tikal Project has unearthed over 100,000 different objects, including tools, ceramics and personal ornaments exhibited at the Sylvanus Morley Museum in the Tikal National Park. Another fascinating museum is the Stelae Museum which, in addition to stelae, displays ceramics, jade objects and other pieces recovered from the archaeological site.

Explorers

In the late 19th century, Modesto Méndez published a report on Tikal that was translated into German. With a series of articles and photographs published at the beginning of the following century, the Austrian Teobert Maler and the Englishman Alfred P. Maudslay brought the archaeological site of Tikal to the world's notice.

Principal Excavations

Between 1914 and 1928, Sylvanus Morley visited the site four times, studying the hieroglyphics and recording the monuments and inscriptions. From 1956 to 1969, the Tikal Project was undertaken by the Museum of Pennsylvania. Between 1972 and 1980, Carlos Rudy Larios and Miguel Orego continued their work. Following the creation of the Tikal National Park, work focused on the Lost World and the Northern Zone.

Altar de Sacrificios

Despite its relatively small size, this site was once the capital of the Rio de la Pasión region. As a result of its position on the shores of this river, it maintained trading links with villages in the highlands of Chiapas and Guatemala. It reached its apogee between A.D. 613 and 771, when construction flourished and the largest number of stelae were built. The last date recorded in this site corresponds to A.D. 910.

El Mirador

Near the border with Mexico, in the north of El Petén, stands the largest Maya archaeological site from the Late pre-Classic, which may hold the key to the origins and nature of the Maya. El Mirador flourished from 150 B.C. to A.D. 250. It contains four groups of triple pyramids (dated *c* A.D. 150); Pava, Structure 34, Danta and El Tigre. From Danta, it is possible to see Nakbé, Río Azul, Tikal and Calakmul (Mexico). The base of El Tigre is six times the area of Temple IV, the largest pyramid in Tikal. The stucco masks in Structure 34 are similar to those of Tikal (Structure 5C-54) and Uaxactún (Structure E-VII-Sub).

Dos Pilas

Late Classic site located in the Río de la Pasión region, notable for its stelae. The Principal Group of the site contains the majority of these carved monuments. The Central Plaza is surrounded by platforms and temples, two of the latter having staircases with hieroglyphics. The Duende Complex is dominated by an enormous platform on a hill. The site contains stelae and defense walls built when the city was besieged in A.D. 761.

Río de la Pasión

The Río de la Pasión basin was the site of many lowland Maya cities that flourished during the Classic. Some of the most important centers, in addition to Ceibal and those in the Petexbatún region, were Itzán, La Amelia, El Caribe and Altar de Sacrificios. The river provided food and served as a trade route, giving power and prosperity to those who lived on its banks.

PIEDRAS NEGRAS

Between A.D. 608 and 810, the ruling elite decided to build stelae at the end of every *hotún* (period of 1,800 days). Through the study of these monuments, seven governors were identified whose hegemony lasted from A.D. 603 to *c* 800. Although the site has been looted, it is still possible to observe Mural 3 (Temple 0-13), the finest bas-relief in the site; Lintel 12 (glyph emblem), with A.D. 514 inscribed on it, making it the monument with the oldest date, while A.D. 795 is the most recently discovered date, and Structure K-5, famous for its mask.

Quiriguá

OTHER AREAS OF GUATEMALA

QUIRIGUÁ

Located a few miles away from the border with Honduras, this city flourished between A.D. 550 and 850 and competed continuously with Copán, (Honduras) which it finally defeated around A.D. 738. It is famous for its immense stelae (one of which is over 33 feet high) and its unusual zoomorphic stones, but the Acropolis, the Great Plaza and the Ceremonial Plaza, all belonging to the Principal Group, are equally important. Quiriguá was declared a World Heritage Site by UNESCO in 1979.

IXIMCHÉ

This city was built during the Post-Classic period, 150 years before the Spanish Conquest. It was the capital of the Cakchiquel nation until 1524 when the conquistadors selected the site to be their first capital. The archaeological site is surrounded by deep valleys and ravines, giving it the aspect of a fortress. All that survives of the ancient city are two ball courts and some small temples.

Iximché

Great Turtle, Quiriguá

ZACULEU

This ceremonial center, two miles from Huehuetenango, in the northern highlands, boasts a series of plazas, stepped pyramids, temples, ball courts and grass-covered mounds. The buildings are plain, with no carved bas-reliefs, friezes or other decoration. There is evidence, however, that the temples were once painted with stucco plaster murals. The most important buildings are Structure I, a 39-foot-high temple with seven tiers which dominates the main plaza, Structure 4, where the ruling elite watched ceremonies from the gallery and Structure 13. The site flourished from A.D. 600 - 1524.

MIXCO VIEJO

Archaeological site that flourished during the Late post-Classic, consisting of temples, palaces on platforms, altars, ballcourts and other buildings. Its buildings attest the wisdom of the Maya in building this city-fortress on a mountain peak that dominates the wild landscape.

EL SALVADOR

Previous page: San Andrés

The largest known settlement in El Salvador is located in Hacienda del Carmen (1400 B.C. -A.D. 250). Demographic growth during the Preclassic fostered local cultural development in Chalchuapa, Santa Leticia and Atiquizaya, which established contacts with Kaminaljuyú in Guatemala. In eastern El Salvador and western Honduras, there was another network of cultural interaction known as the "Uapala ceramic sphere." The havoc caused by the eruption of the Ilopango Volcano led to the occupation of the area until the Late Classic by villages such as San Andrés in the Valle of Zapotitán. Nevertheless, Tazumal, located to the south of Chalchuapa, continued as the most important center of the Classic period. The first migrations of Pipiles (Nahuas) took place during the Post-Classic and the immigrants settled in Cihuatán and Santa María.

SAN ANDRÉS

Ceremonial center from the late Classic, set on a fertile plain between the San Salvador volcano and the Lamatepec mountain range. Although still only partially excavated, archaeologists working at the site have unearthed a pyramid, in addition to other buildings. The large number of "scent caskets" used to transport cinnabar and iron oxide discovered at the site support the idea that San Andrés played a significant role in the region's trade.

JOYA DE CERÉN

This is the finest example of an ancient Mayan farming village. Approximately 1,400 years ago, the eruption of the Laguna Caldera volcano buried this village which was preserved under 20 feet of volcanic ash. Excavation began in 1989, some of the most important findings being adobe houses and kitchens with petrified food that was being prepared at the time of the catastrophe. Knives, obsidian axes, grinding stones, jade beads and carved deer bones have also been found.

Joya de Cerén

TAZUMAL

Between 300 B.C .and A.D. 1200, the area where this site is located was a key cultural center. Tazumal ("place of many lakes" in Náhuatl) contains a ball court and a 100-foot-high pyramid. Excavations of the pyramid uncovered 20 Classic tombs and 320 ceramic objects. The nearby palace was a cemetery for the sovereigns of Tazumal.

Tazumal

H O N D

U R A S

In approximately 5000 B.C., settlements linked to semi-sedentary groups were recorded in the Sula Valley. By 1000 B.C., the Copán area (Sepulturas and El Bosque) was inhabited by farmers who also produced ceramics. In the Motagua River basin, two principal centers emerged: Copán and Quiriguá (in Guatemala). Copán experienced its greatest urban growth between A.D. 400 and 900, as a result of its trade monopoly on obsidian and jade from the Guaytán deposits. In the mid-7th century, the thirteenth governor of Copán, 18-Rabbit, was defeated by Cauac Sky, Lord of Quiriguá, who thereafter controlled the resources of Lake Izabal and the port of Nito , on the River Dulce, points of access to the Caribbean coastal routes. The post-Classic (900-1500) was marked by the links between the Sula Valley and the Valley of Mexico.

El Puente

EL PUENTE

Archaeological zone located near the village of La Entrada, on the turn-off from the western highway, on the way to Copán. This is the second most important archaeological site in Honduras, after Copán. El Puente was opened to the public in 1994.

Las Sepulturas was the residential area of the elite, so-called because of the Mayan custom of burying their dead in the house where they lived

Altar G1, Copán

Stelae C & F, Great Plaza, Copan

Altar, Copan

COPÁN

The first settlements in the Copán valley date from 1200 B.C. and its abandonment occurred during the 9th century. The principal structure is the Acropolis, which is divided into two large plazas. In the east plaza stands Temple 11, erected by Yax Pac, its last ruler; it is also the site of Altar Q. Temple 16 was built on top of an earlier temple. The ballcourt is one of the finest in the Maya World; its markers in the shape of a macaw's head are particularly striking. The Hieroglyphic Staircase of Structure 10L-26 contains the longest hieroglyphic text in the Maya World, with over 1,250 blocks of inscriptions.

The Great Plaza contains stelae and statues with distinctive zoomorphic features. Other important structures are the Rosalila temple and the Papagayo complex. Las Sepulturas was the residential area of the elite, so-called because of the Maya custom of burying their dead in the house where they lived.

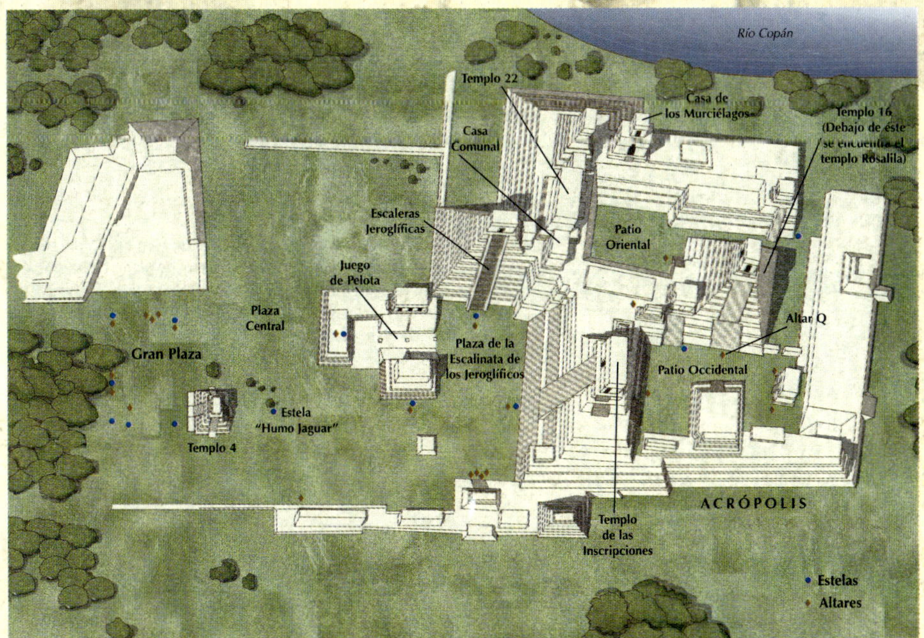

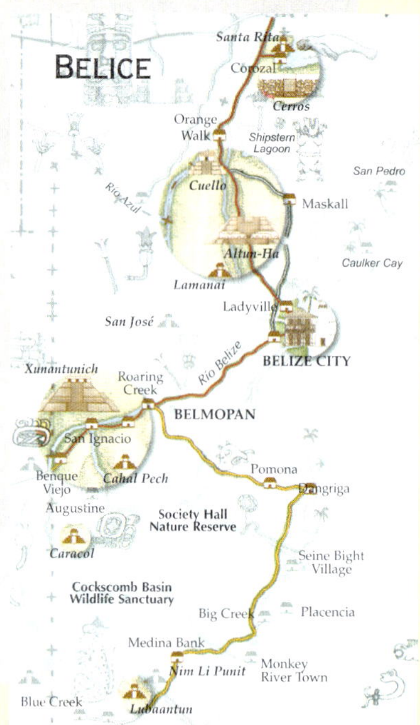

(Cont. Yucatán)

•**IZAMAL** 52 km from Mérida on highway 180 via Kantunil; then 18 km north. Visiting time: 2 hours.

•**EK BALAM** 180 km from Mérida on highway 180 via Valladolid; continue north on highway 295 towards Tizimín.

•**DZIBILCHALTÚN** 14 km from Mérida on highway 261. Visiting time: 2 hours.

•**UXMAL** 80 km from Mérida on highway 261. Visiting time: 2 hours.

•**KABAH** 103 km from Mérida on highway 261. Visiting time: 1 hour.

•**SAYIL** 113 km from Mérida on highway 261. Visiting time: 30 minutes.

•**XLAPAK** 118 km from Mérida on highway 261. Visiting time: 30 minutes.

•**LABNÁ** 22 km from Mérida on highways, 261, 184 and 31. Visiting time: 30 minutes.

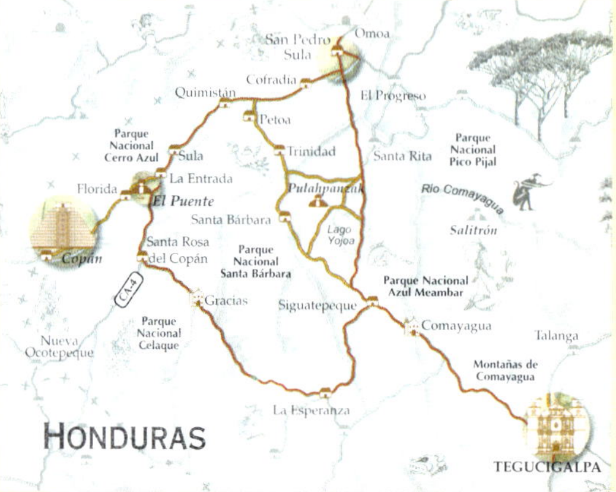

•**OXKINTOK** 73 km from Mérida on highway 180 via Maxcanú; from there, go southeast on highway 184. Visiting time: 1 hour.

•**ACANCEH** 45 minutes from Mérida on highway 180. Visiting time: 30 minutes.

•**MAYAPÁN** 47 km from Mérida on highway 180 via Acanceh and Tecoh. Visiting time: 1 hour.

•**LOLTÚN** 134 km from Mérida on highway 261; the site is 20 km after Labná. Visiting time: 3 hours.

•**AKÉ** 30 km from Mérida on highway 172 via Tixcocob. Visiting time: 30 minutes.

•**CHACMULTÚN** From Mérida to Muná on highway 261; continue on highway 184 to Oxkutzcab and Tekax, then from Tekax on foot to the site.

BELIZE

•**ALTÚN HA** 45 km north of Belize City on the old northern highway that passes through Sand Hill and Lucky Strike. Visiting time: 2 hours.

•**CERROS** Located at the northern tip of Belize, close to Chetumal Bay, Mexico. The best way to get there is from Corozal, where boats can be hired to take you to the site.

•**LAMANAI** 56 km from Orange Walk, in northern Belize. Reached by boat along the New River. Visiting time: 2 hours.

•**CARACOL** South of San Ignacio in western Belize. Can be reached by car from San Ignacio or Belize City. Visiting time: 1 day, including transportation time.

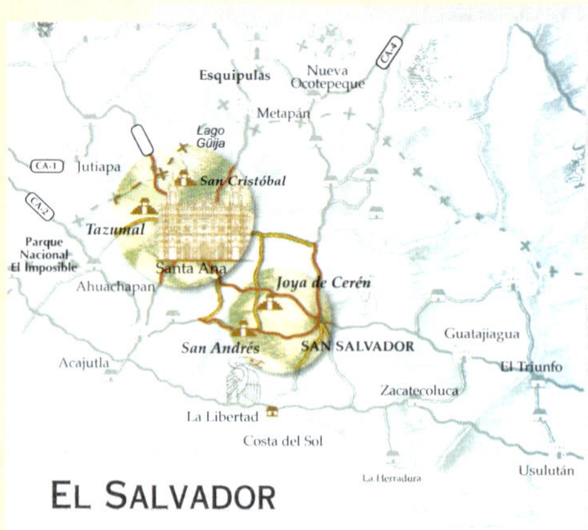

•**XUNANTUNICH** 128 km from Belize City, close to the border with Guatemala. Reached by crossing the River Mopán in a ferry at San José Succotz, 16 km from San Ignacio. Visiting time: 2 hours.

•**LUBAANTÚN** Located a few km north of San Ignacio Columbia, to the northwest of Punta Gorda in southern Belize. Visiting time: 1 hour.

•**SANTA RITA** Most of the site is buried under the modern town of Corozal, in northern Belize. Visiting time: half an hour.

•**CUELLO** Northwest of Belize City in the direction of Orange Walk; at km 30.5 is the track leading to the site. Visiting time: 1 hour.

•**CAHAL PECH** 3 km from San Ignacio, western Belize. Reached on foot or on horseback along paths from San Ignacio; alternatively, on the highway from Belize City.

HONDURAS

•**COPÁN** 438 km from Tegucigalpa and 184 km from San Pedro Sula. Reached from Tegucigalpa on highway CA-7; from San Pedro Sula by the highway to Comayagua. There are flights from Guatemala City as well as charter flights from Tegucigalpa and San Pedro Sula. Visiting time: 3 hours.

•**EL PUENTE**
Located near La Entrada, on highway CA-11. Visiting time: 2 hours.

EL SALVADOR

•**SAN ANDRÉS** Drive 35 km west of San Salvador on the Panamerican Highway, as far as the junction indicating the site entrance. Visiting time: 2 hours.

•**JOYA DE CERÉN** From San Salvador take the Panamerican Highway to San Andrés; the site is 5 km further on. Visiting time 2 hours.

•**TAZUMAL** 15 km west of Santa Ana, in the Chalchuapa archaeological zone. Visiting time: 3 hours.

GUATEMALA

•**ZACULEU** 5 km from Huehuetenango; take the main road west. Visiting time: 2 hours.

•**SANTA LUCÍA COTZUMALGUAPA** 4 km from Escuintla. Hire a guide and obtain permission to visit the property. Visiting time: 2 hours.

•**MONTE ALTO-LA DEMOCRACIA** On the Pacific coast in the province of Escuintla, southwest of Guatemala City. By road via Escuintla and Siquinala. Visiting time: 2 hours.

•**ABAJ TAKALIK** On the outskirts of Retalhuleu. From Guatemala City via Sololá and Quetzaltenango, then turn south to Retalhuleu. Visiting time: 2 hours.

•**TIKAL** 64 km from the city of Flores. The road trip from Guatemala City takes 12 hours. Also reached from Chetumal (Mexico) via Belize. The air trip in a small plane from Guatemala City takes 30 minutes to Santa Elena (Flores). There are regular flights to Santa Elena from Cancún. Visiting time: 1 day.

•**UAXACTÚN** 89 km from Flores; a dirt road in good condition links the site with Tikal, 40 km away. Visiting time: 3 hours.

•**YAXHÁ** 30 km southeast of Tikal. From Flores take the highway that passes through Ixlú and is bound for El Remate and Melchor de Mencos. At La Máquina (37 km) turn north for 11 km. Visiting time: 1 day.

•**TOPOXTÉ** Located on an island in Lake Yaxhá, and reached by boat from El Remate. Visiting time: 1 day.

•**NAKUM** 25 km east of Tikal and 17 km north of Yaxhá. Reached on horseback or in a four-wheel drive vehicle via Yaxhá. Visiting time: half a day including transportation time.

•**NARANJO** Plan the visit from Yaxhá, hiring a guide. Visiting time: 1 day including transportation time.

•**RÍO AZUL** Located near the Mexican border, 80 km from Tikal and 110 km from Flores. The best route is Flores-Uaxactún-Ixcanrio, in a four-wheel drive vehicle . Ixcanrio is next to the river, very close to the site. Visiting time: 1 day.

Each visit to a Mayan archaeological site is a journey back through time

•**EL MIRADOR** 7 km from the Mexican border. Plan your visit from Flores. A guide is essential. Visiting time: 3 hours.

•**CEIBAL** 12 km east of Sayaxché. Reached by dirt road or along the La Pasión River. Visiting time: 2 hours.

•**PIEDRAS NEGRAS** Reached by the Usumacinta River, after navigating along the La Pasión River from Sayaxché. Only accessible during the dry season. Visiting time: transportation and tour take at least two days. Visitors may camp on the banks of the river.

•**QUIRIGUÁ** 208 km from Guatemala City, by highway CA-9. On reaching Los Amates, follow the signs to the site. Visiting time: 3 hours.

•**DOS PILAS** Located between the La Pasión and Usumacinta rivers, close to Sayaxché. Reached by boat along the Chacrío River, a tributary of La Pasión. Visiting time: 1 hour.

•**AGUATECA** Southeast of Dos Pilas, on the banks of Lake Petén Petexbatún. A guide is essential. Visiting time: 1 hour.

•**ALTAR DE SACRIFICIOS** East of Ceibal, very near the Usumacinta River, on the border with Mexico. Reached by boat along the La Pasión River. Visiting time: 1 hour.

•**KAMINALJUYÚ** The vestiges of this site are located in Guatemala City. Visiting time: 1 hour.

•**MIXCO VIEJO** Close to Guatemala City, but access is not easy. Advisable to hire a guide and a four-wheel drive vehicle in the city. Visiting time: 1 day including transportation.

•**IXIMCHÉ** Located a few km west of Lake Atitlán. Visiting time: 2 hours.

Zoomorph, Quiriguá, Guatemala

MUSEUMS IN THE MAYA WORLD

The museums in the area showcase stunning examples of Mayan art. Major archaeological sites such as Palenque, Uxmal, Chichén Itzá, Copán and Tikal have site museums.

CAMPECHE

Museo Regional de Campeche
Fuerte de San Miguel, Campeche

CHIAPAS

Museo Regional de Chiapas
Calzada de los Hombres Ilustres
s/n Fracc. Madero, Tuxtla Gutiérrez

Museo de Los Altos de Chiapas
Exconvento de Santo Domingo,
San Cristóbal de Las Casas

QUINTANA ROO

Museo de la Cultura Maya
Av. Héroes s/n, Chetumal

Museo de Antropología e Historia
Next to the Convention Center,
Hotel Zone, Cancún

Museo de la Isla de Cozumel
Rafael E. Melgar, between calles 4 & 6 Norte, Cozumel

TABASCO

Museo Regional de Antropología
"Carlos Pellicer Cámara"
Periférico Carlos Pellicer Cámara
No. 511
Zona CICOM, Villahermosa

Parque-Museo La Venta
Av. Ruiz Cortines 5 min. from the Hotel Zone and Tabasco 2000
Villahermosa

YUCATÁN

Museo Regional de Antropología
Paseo Montejo, between calles 41 & 43, Mérida

Museo del Pueblo Maya
Dzibilchaltún archaeological site

EL SALVADOR

Museo Nacional de Historia
Southeast of Saburo Hirao Park, en route to the Zoo
Barrio Modelo, San Salvador

Museo de Joya de Cerén
Joya de Cerén archaeological site,
La Libertad province.

GUATEMALA

Museo Nacional de Antropología y Etnología
Edificio No. 5, Finca La Aurora,
Zona 13, Guatemala City

Museo Popol Vuh
6a. Calle Final, Zona 10, Campus de la Universidad Francisco Marroquín, Guatemala City

HONDURAS

Museo Nacional de Antropología e Historia
Barrio Villa Roy, Tegucigalpa